A POUND OF EXPERIENCE, A PINCH OF HUMOR

LIZ SWIERTZ NEWMAN

Versions of some stories herein were previously published in *A Community of Voices; Tiny Lights, Searhlights & Signal Flares; Coast Magazine;* and *The Daily Pilot,* a Community Newspaper of *The Los Angeles Times.* Some of the stories have not been published previously, partly because I hate marketing.

The author warrants full ownership of and/or legal rights to publish all the materials in this book.

The opinions expressed in this book are solely the opinions of the author—or maybe of others but as construed by the author—and no one but the author should be held accountable for them. Any errors are my own, and as the old saying goes, "Only Buddha is perfect."

You may contact the author at Liz@LSNewman.com. If you're a single male in your 70s, play duplicate bridge, and live in her neck of the woods, she will for sure return your e.

ISBN-13: 978-1548181543
ISBN-10: 1548181544

An old Polish adage—which I am by birth entitled to use—is a reminder not to get involved in emotional dramas that don't concern us: "Not my circus. Not my monkeys." (A good device, though it doesn't work well for me.)

Dedicated to all my monkeys—

The McNewgans

Mark, Tim, Bobby & Britt, Cheryl, Jan, Brian, Monica, Teresa, Maura, Kath, Colleen, Sharon

"You are the landlord of your own head.
Don't let others rent space there
if they aren't going to be good tenants."

~ *Holiday Mathis*

TABLE OF CONTENTS

PREFACE i

Part I, Part 1

NOT PREVIOUSLY PUBLISHED 1

Part I, Part 2

AN ELEVEN O'CLOCK SCHOLAR 21
From My BA & Master's Classes 23

Part II, Part 1

PREVIOUSLY PUBLISHED 43
From *Coast Magazine* 45
From *A Community of Voices*. 47
From Tiny Lights. 71

Part II, Part 2

PREVIOUSLY PUBLISHED, REVISITED. 73
From *The Daily Pilot*. 75

ACKNOWLEDGMENTS 231

PREFACE

Welcome to *A Pound of Experience, A Pinch of Humor*. Except for Part I, Part 2, these stories represent much of what I have written since I was 74, not counting books. Or emails.

My wish is that, as you read the stories, you'll discover that our experiences are similar, that we are not all that different at any age, and even that growing older might have its appeal.

If you're a youngster (under 65), I'd like you to end up believing that when you're 77, that's not going to be so old.

Business:

In some references, I italicize the LA Times and the Daily Pilot, but I've decided not to do it in the stories. Or the Preface. When you write your book, do whatever you like.

In Part II, Part 2, the stories previously published in the Daily Pilot, I used both my title and the Pilot's headline, unless they were similar, in which case I used just my title.

In the Pilot stories, names of books are in quotation marks. We all know they should be underlined or in all-caps or italics, but newspapers don't use underlining or all-caps or italics. I did use those devices in the stories as revised herein, but I left titles in the newspaper format.

Another thing newspapers don't use is the "Oxford comma." I do use the Oxford comma. If you don't know what it is, you can Google it, and you'll feel very smart. You might discover that you use the Oxford comma yourself!

I sincerely hope you enjoy the book and give a copy as a gift to everyone you know.

All best,
Liz Swiertz Newman

P.S. If you're a guy, don't think this is "a chick book" just because the first two stories are women-oriented.

Part I, Part 1

NOT PREVIOUSLY PUBLISHED

One Waxed Leg

Once upon a time in a land far north of here, there was a woman, finished raising small children, who decided to put on her big-girl panties (before that was even a saying) and do what other women regularly do.

I was in my middle forties before I even called myself a woman, so it was at about that time.

I lived up the street from a *place de beauté*, and convenience has always motivated me, even though it took about ten years for it to motivate me in this case. But time and tide eventually coincided, and I made an appointment for a leg-waxing.

I didn't know how leg-waxing was supposed to work. (1) Is it like tidying up before the housekeepers come? Or (2) is it like being obsessive-compulsive and cleaning the toilet with a toothbrush before the housekeepers come? Or (3) is it like *I haven't cleaned this place in a month. Have at it.*

What woman actually enjoys shaving her legs? The other options of de-fuzzing one's legs are limited. Depilatories are messy and smelly (I'm told). Electrolysis would be expensive as well as time consuming. I once went with my friend Maggie to get just her forearms eloctrolysized, and it's a good thing I took a book!

Leg-waxing was becoming common back then—meaning it had finally crossed my radar. It might still be. It's not a subject that comes up much in my circle of friends. The older we get, the less hairy we are. It's one of the golden benefits of aging.

We of Polish descent are generally not very hairy people to begin with. I was 15 before I began shaving my legs. My brother-in-law told me it was time.

I asked my sister. "Is it time? Pete says it's time."

Carolyn said that if Pete said it's time, it's probably

time. "He's saying it from a guy's point-of-view."

So I accepted that girls' leg-shaving had something to do with guys' points-of-viewing.

And I dutifully shaved regularly for most of my life, like my mother before me and my daughters after me. Although, in the 1970s, one of my daughters asked me what I would say if she told me she had stopped shaving her legs, and I answered, "Don't show me your armpits."

But the idea of not *shaving* legs had its appeal, sort of like nice/not nice. According to my husband Lee, he didn't care whether or not I shaved my legs, so I tended to not shave all that often. But come to think of it, he might have meant it situationally, as in "I don't care if you haven't shaved your legs!"

I'd heard lots of women say "I had my legs waxed today . . . Oh, and a Brazilian on my 'hoo-haw.'" Wait . . . Women wax their hoo-haws?

Hmm. A *Brazilian*. Maybe the girls from Ipanema are genetically hirsute and need a trim before they don their bikinis.

I deactivated the visuals in my head.

Once I'd done all that processing (and procrastinating) and had all those discussions with myself (and procrastinated some more), "it was time" when I went down the hill to the place where I would join the forces of women internationally and get my legs waxed.

Ahh, warm wax spread over my leg. Ahh, the gentle pressure of the aesthetician's hands as she affixed strips atop the wax. And then, r-r-r-i-p!

AAAAAAAAAAAAAACK! Stop, stop, stop! STOP!

Tears were streaming down my face from the pain. Holy shitzkie! That must be what a building feels like when it's being sand-blasted.

The aesthetician said, "Oh, that's the worst of it, dear. If you've never had this done before, that first removal does come as a surprise. But now you're used to it, and the rest won't hurt like that."

She didn't believe it either. I know because she ripped, ripped, ripped all the strips off my leg as fast as she could, while I screamed.

I didn't let her wax the other leg.

I went home and Vaselined the owie leg and shaved the other one.

And so, it will be . . . it will be the *end of never* before I'll have another leg waxed. Or anything else.

If, according to our current president (2017), an interrogator should use torture on a prisoner with alleged knowledge of terrorists, he should have the questioner wax one leg of that suspect. He'll find out anything he wants with just a promise not to wax that second leg.

If no information is forthcoming, threaten him with a Brazilian.

If still no intel, the guy knows *nothing!* Let him go!

• • •

Pranx, but NO Pranx

"You aren't wearing a sweatshirt today," Jeanne said. Jeanne is my childhood friend who 70 years later is again my neighbor.

We were having lunch at a local bistro. "It's a nice place," I said. "I tried to dress to the occasion."

But Jeanne's comment reminded me of a conversation we'd had about a year earlier. I'd told her that one reason I wear sweatshirts is that I'm self-conscious about my accumulated bulges, and she'd asked if I'd ever heard of Pranx.

"I've never heard of pranks as a solution to bulges," I said.

Jeanne laughed. "No, Pranx is . . . an undergarment that holds in the bulges. You can buy them just for your midriff area or for from your midriff to your knees."

"You mean like control-top panty hose? Because those don't work above the waistline. They barely work below the waistline."

"Well, no. There is significantly more control than that," she said. "Try them! I believe Nordstrom carries them."

I didn't ask Jeanne how she knew that. There are some questions that even best friends don't ask.

I filed the idea away. I thought about Pranx from time to time, probably whenever I wasn't wearing a sweatshirt.

I almost always wear sweatshirts. Besides being comfy, they conceal creepy arm-crepe, emerging gene-inheritance, and moderate overindulgence. There are more than a dozen sweatshirts in my closet. OK, more than two dozen.

But Jeanne had told me, after Lee and I moved here—the first time I asked her what I should wear somewhere—"It's Newport Beach. We don't dress up much in Newport Beach." I took her at her word.

The day did arrive, however, when my mood to try on Pranx

intersected Nordie's lingerie department. I whispered my request to the saleswoman and said that I thought I would take a large.

Alone in the dressing room, I looked at the long, narrow, stretchy fabric. I checked to confirm that it *was* a large or whether the woman, by chance, had pulled an extra small from the rack.

With a sigh, I removed my shoes and jeans and sweatshirt and began to pull on what reminded me of an elastic bandage I once had for a sore elbow. Each leg was about as big.

I was going to have to do this sitting down.

OK, so maybe I needed an extra large. I stuck my head out and called "Miss!" And back she came with an extra large, showing no judgment in her expression.

I sat down. I slipped my foot into the right leg. I slipped my foot into the left leg. I thought, maybe if I had some baby powder, or some Vaseline. I pulled. Up one calf. Up the other calf. I stood. I pulled. I gripped tighter and yanked. I sat. I took my foot out of the left leg and focused on my right leg, easing my thumbs to the bottom and stretching the fabric wide.

When I got the garment to my knees, I realized Pranx is just a full-body tourniquet.

Call me a quitter.

These should be called "Pranx, but no thanks," I thought. Only women who don't need them could possibly get them on.

I got dressed and returned the undergarment to the saleswoman. "This didn't work for me," I said.

"Is there anything else I can help you with?" she asked.

"Yes," I answered. "If you have a sweatshirt department."

• • •

New Phone

Two of our kids, Cheryl and Bobby, wanted me to get all new phones after their father died. The kind that identify callers, etc.

All new phones? Phfffft. Just *one* of my phones was funky and needed to be replaced.

The "Set-up and Use" directions for my new $39.99 two-line desk phone consist of both sides of a paper that measures 16 inches by 24 inches, folded in sixths and then in thirds, printed in 8-point sans-serif font.

Thirty-two 3-inch by 5-inch unreadable, indecipherable tissue-like pages.

I threw the instructions in with my recycling. All my phone has to do is let me dial out and answer it.

With my previous new phone, I plugged in the ends of the cord that connects to the phone and to the wall jack, and the ends of the coil cord that connects to the phone and to the handset, and *voilá!* So that's what I did with this one.

Punch the buttons and make a call, or answer the ring by picking up the handset and saying "Hello there!"

Technology can march on without me—even if my next over-achieving telephone comes with a speaker, caller ID, call waiting, conference-calling, message notification, redial, call storage, speed-dial, and a read-out screen that does everything but spit out info like a ticker-tape.

Hmm. Do ticker-tapes even still exist?

• • •

Aside

I can't resist the urge to compare the big five-cent bar of candy when I was a child to the "double bars" now sold. Candy bars got smaller and smaller as the prices rose higher and higher. Without doubling the bars, the next size reduction/price increase would have resulted in bar candy the size of a piece of See's selling for a couple bucks.

Wait. A piece of See's probably *sells* for a couple bucks! When we moved to California in 1945, it was a dollar a pound.

Hence the big box of "bite size" candy sold at the movies—smaller even than "Halloween-size" treats.

If my sister and brother and I wanted a piece of chewing gum, my mother gave us Beeman's Pepsin because it was good for our digestion. I remember its jingle, too. "Gimme a package of Beeman's Pepsin chewing gum, please!"

Pepsin didn't taste good. As a result, we didn't often want gum and grew up without the gum-chewing habit.

And, frankly, although I think it's a kick to chew gum and noisily snap it, it looks disgusting when someone else does it.

Nevertheless, considering what Americans pay annually for antacids and heartburn meds—$10 billion according to the Internet—maybe Mr. Beeman should market his gum to the general public again. (It *is* currently available in catalogs featuring "nostalgia" items.)

Instead of in a box like Chicklets, it could sell in airy double sticks, for ten times the price of a single "chickle."

• • •

A Phone Call from out of this World

The most amazing thing happened. I received a phone call from my husband! I'd never dreamed I'd hear from him again.

"Where are you?" I asked.

"In heaven, of course. Was there ever any doubt?" Lee said.

"Of course not, but . . . how . . . ? Gosh, it's great to hear your voice, honey. It's been two and a half years!"

"Time flies in eternity. What's a day for us might be ten days for you—maybe more. I don't know. I don't get the daily newspaper up here. Hah-hah."

I laughed too. "Well . . . what *do* you do all day?"

"Today I had my class in Criminal Law . . . "

I was astonished. "You have criminals in heaven?"

"Oh, no, no," he said. "But, you know that I always wanted to be a lawyer, and we can do whatever we want up here. That's what heaven is."

"Wow. That's phenomenal. Uh, what else do you do up there?"

"Let's see. Some of us guys from my WWII cadets' class have a poker game about once a . . . once a *whatever*."

"Uh, say Hi to Troy and Chuck for me. What about God. Have you seen God?" I asked.

"Oh, yeah. He's a great guy. We can see him whenever we like. A while back, I took him some lilies-of-the-valley I grew."

"Oh, you're gardening again! Your back doesn't hurt anymore! You must be in . . . I was going to say 'heaven.'" We both laughed.

"I can grow those things you loved in Kansas that I couldn't grow in California. Oh! Tell Bobby I'm golfing again. Quite a respectable score, too. I haven't been at it for long. Up here, time is sort of elastic—whatever you need it to be."

"That's all just wondrous. Oh! Honey, did you go through a white-light tunnel when you died? Like we hear about?"

"Yes, yes, I did. And my parents were here to greet me! Imagine that! It was amazing. They look like they're in their fifties. My Dad never even reached his fifties! I think you see people here in some relation to your life, whatever that is. Not sure how old I look. Maybe different to different people. It doesn't matter. Everybody whoever knew you knows who you are. And vice versa."

"This is incredible, Lee. No one is going to believe that you called me!"

"You might want to keep it to yourself, or maybe yourself and . . . oh, say Hi to the kids."

"Are you kidding? I am going to tell everybody!"

"OK, but be prepared for the reactions."

"You mean like when I was called a blasphemer in Gelson's parking lot—because of my bumper sticker about the Lord not owning a gun?" I asked.

"Not like that so much. Some people will think you're crazy, of course. And everyone else is going to want to know if you asked me this and asked me that, and you'll be unhappy that you didn't think of it during our chat, and you'll end up almost sorry you told *anyone*," he said.

"But not sorry you called, honey! I am thrilled."

"Golly, it's good to hear my Lizzie's voice. Almost makes me wish I were back in Corona del Mar. But I was so darn uncomfortable with my earthly afflictions. I'll just wait here for you."

"Sorry about that. I pretty much expect to be down here until I'm 120. You know how long-lived my parents were," I said.

"Whatever it takes, sweetheart. Uh-oh. You're starting to break up . . . "

"I love you!" I shouted over the crackle.

"I love you, too," Lee said. "Take your time. We'll have eternity together."

And then, just like that, he was gone. But I was left with the most positive feelings! Not sad at all. Glad for him. Glad for me.

Glad for eternity.

• • •

Passing Down My Heirlooms

I still have my Girl Scout pin. I still have my little blue-enameled perfect-Mass-attendance pin from grammar school. I still have my college sorority lavalier and pin. But I don't have my high school class ring. And that's a wondrous thing!

It was such a thrill when, as juniors at Immaculate Heart High, we received our class rings! We especially liked wearing it to our prom and the boys' proms and flashing it as we flicked ashes from our cigarettes. We were so grown up and worldly. We thought.

Except for our initials inside—mine, the unenviable monogram MES—all class rings were the same: IHHS on one side and the year on the other, and in the center, either a black or a blue square stone with a flower-wreathed heart, pierced by a sword—the Immaculate Heart for which my school was named—a symbol of the pain the Blessed Mother suffered at the horrid death of her son.

I thought it was kind of creepy as a class ring, and I only wore it for my junior and senior years. Then it went into my jewelry box with my other trinket-memories.

Until my niece Teresa, the fifth of my sister's six daughters who went to IHHS, asked if she could wear it.

Wow. Yes, I liked having it in its little velvet square, but what would I ever do with it? It wouldn't mean anything to my sons. So, of course I gave my almost-25-year-old class ring to Teresa. And she didn't wear it just for two years in high school. She wore it for longer than it sat in my jewelry box!

Then one day, Teresa's second cousin Irene (on her father's side) became a junior at IHHS. When Teresa asked if she could give "our" ring to Irene, that relationship sounded traditional enough to me.

14

Yes! Of course, she *must!*

Passing a ring down through nieces is something of a custom in my family. My mother's sister, my Aunt Babe, gave me her childhood signet ring with an M on it. (I was 12 before I knew her name was Martha and not Babe.) My aunt had only sons, and back then I was called by my full name, Mary Elizabeth. So I got to have the M ring.

And I loved that ring and wore it until it was too small for my littlest finger, well into my twenties. And into the jewel box it went (with my high school ring).

Then my sister's daughter Maura was a little girl about as old as I was when Aunt Babe gave me her ring, and I passed the ring along to Maura, who was able to wear it for such a long, long time on her slim fingers.

Her younger sister Monica didn't get the ring, but when Monica's daughter Maude was a little girl, Maude received my aunt's signet ring, with the understanding that she would pass it along to her own niece one day. She has a little sister who might have a daughter named Marian or Marin, or she'll marry someone who's sibling has a little girl named Marla or Marietta.

And all the nieces who wore my aunt's ring, and all the girls who wore my class ring will have this lovely continuum!

. . .

Getting Our Kicks from Route 15 to Route 66

You don't need to fly, cross borders, or take excessive time away from normal life to enjoy a fun-filled, sight-satisfying and perhaps unusual Easter vacation.

Son Mark and I recently saw much of Arizona in just four days, not counting a three-day visit in Wickenburg with favorite cousins, Carole, Ron, and Jackie. Wickenburg is a sweet, small town, with all the modern conveniences (e.g., hospital, library, supermarket, golf course, theater) and five life-size, talking, Western-era-themed vignettes.

On Wednesday, Mark and I headed toward Scottsdale to see Frank Lloyd Wright's installation, Taliesen West.

Lee and I had visited Wright's concrete Hollywood masterpieces, the Hollyhock and Storer houses. They bear *zero* resemblance to Taliesen West!

Wright's winter home and architectural school was built in 1937. From petroglyphs and Chinese figurines as exterior points of interest, to its native-rock, metal, canvas, and glass construction, Taliesen West defies description. You'll just have to see it yourselves!

Wright lived there and accepted commissions until his death at the age of 91—leaving 500 unfinished projects.

Mark and I raced from there to Sedona. Our sensations as we approached its red rock outcroppings reminded us of our first glimpse of Mount Rushmore in 1977. Just . . . breathtaking! Around each bend were more phenomenal shapes and colors, until we were surrounded by magnificence.

I must note that while in Sedona, we dined at two excellent restaurants: Judi's, which was within walking distance of our Best Western, and Sound Bites, which featured brilliant guitar stylist Anthony Mazzella.

We did most of our sight-seeing on Thursday. In addition to galleries, shops, and New Age centers, Sedona is noted for its healing electrical vortexes.

Margareth, our tour guide, took us to a chapel near a vortex. While I waited for Mark to show her something he'd seen inside, I seem to have zoned out.

"Oh, there you are," I said, startled to see they'd returned.

"We've been watching you for several minutes," Margareth said.

I'd been deep in thought, but . . . ?

James, the hotel driver who'd shuttled us to the best viewing site the previous evening, had pointed out the airport vortex. He said he'd climbed the hill, placed his hand on a rock, and felt palpitations in his heart and throughout his body. "But," James added, "I'm an old man who had just climbed a hill."

So, make of our experiences what you will.

Friday morning we headed to Jerome, which well-met tourists Becky and Paul (from Fond du Lac, Wisconsin) raved about. First stop, Nelly Bly's for kaleidoscopes and paperweights.

Jerome is a jewel of a ghost-inhabited mining town, although our spirit-energy detectors didn't flash while we ghost-toured the area. After three hours' of fascinating history and sightseeing, our-guide Scott told us to visit the Catholic church, where he'd had a ghostly encounter.

Something weird did happen there. I'd stepped into an alcove where the confessionals were. I was surprised to see evergreen branches sticking out from beneath the velvet-curtains. I called to Mark. "Look at this!"

As I turned toward him, I heard a woman say "Look at this!"

"Who said that?" I asked. "I heard someone say 'Look at this.'"

"*You* said it," Mark answered.

We tried to make an echo occur, without success. I swear I heard what I'd said repeated, and I'm going with the Ghost of
Easter Present.

We spent the night in Jerome's Grand Hotel, a giant building that during its 90 years has served as hospital, school, sanitarium, miners' housing, and finally a hotel—also haunted. But our most out-of-this-world experience occurred in the hotel's restaurant, the Asylum. The names and flavors of the food and drinks, the service and the presentation—all were positively heavenly.

We were off by 8:00 on Saturday to make our way home via Route 66. Y'all remember "Kingman, Barstow, San Bernardino!"

I'd ridden Route 66 to Los Angeles in 1945, when my father was transferred from Kansas to the West Coast. Not so many towns now, but lots of wildflowers, Saguaro cactus, "jumping cholla," and Burma-Shave signs!

In some stretches, Burma-Shave signs come up every five miles or less, in their sets of five. Here's an example I remember from 1945: The spring has sprung . . . The grass has riz . . . Where last year's . . . Careless driver is. . . . Burma Shave.

We continued our ongoing souvenir-overload in Seligman and Oatman.

Seligman's Roadkill Café provided a delightful menu. My patty melt was called "Tried-to-pass-me-by-on-rye." We loaded up on Route 66 memorabilia at the Roadrunner.

In Oatman, wild burros have the right-of-way. They are allowed to roam freely, and one followed Mark into a souvenir shop. (The proprietor gently ushered it out.)

The Oatman Hotel featured excellent ice cream and a view of the room where Clark Gable and Carol Lombard honeymooned. In its restaurant/bar, all vertical and horizontal surfaces are covered with autographed one-dollar bills—millions of them! Though defaced with signatures.

After a short while in Oatman, the shadows grew long, and we were eager to resume freeway speed.

We zigged from the I-40 for dinner at Peggy Sue's '50s Diner in Yerma (my friends Susan and John told me about that charming anachronism). After dinner, we did a walk-through of our last gift shop, then headed south on the I-15, arriving home in two hours.

I can't get from Newport Beach to Tarzana in two hours!

The world never goes on hold while I'm away: phone calls, emails, and snail mail pile up. Luggage doesn't unpack itself or do laundry. Souvenirs don't unwrap and place themselves.

Ghost wanted.

• • •

The Grieving Season

I first noticed it last year
Relative to the deaths of my two people most dear:
My sister Carolyn had rocketed beyond the sky
Five years ago, on the Fourth of July;
And Lee, two years after, on a date I'll always remember,
The sixth of September. And our anniversary's in November.
And so for months last year and also this year,
Constantly, beneath each eyelid loomed a tear.

I'm telling you this—not to make you sad—but for a reason:
There's such a thing as "the grieving season."
For all my life when someone died, I'd send flowers,
And that was that. (Only one had cried with me for hours).
I never thought that on *their* birthdays they'd be sad,
Or on their anniversaries they'd be glad
If I called to say
"I'm thinking of you and [your loved one] today."

When someone asked how *I* was doing, "Fine"
Was the answer I'd learned from others, and their
    answer became mine.
How much easier to smile and deceive—
And "Fine" be what our good-hearted friends believe—
Than make them all feel creepy
By being weepy.
And if you find *yourself* feeling sad for no reason,
Could it be your grieving season?

• • •

An Abecedarian
of What I Should Have Told My Kids

Acknowledge all incoming good.
Buy new stuff you like, not what matches
the old stuff you don't you don't like.
Close the door and move on when it's over.
Donate time or money to honorable causes or charities.
Excuses aren't the same as reasons.
Follow your dreams.
Go out and play, even as an adult.
Hydrate yourself and the littlies.
Ink comes out if you soak it in milk,
unless it's permanent ink.
Just say "Sorry, no" if you don't want to or don't have time.
Know it for sure or look it up before you share it
(www.snopes.com).
Learn something new: e.g., Italian, bridge, harmonica.
Measure twice; cut once. (That would be from Dad.)
Negotiate to agreement.
Open the windows and air out your house every week.
Put yourself in the other guy's flip flops.
Quarantine yourself if you need time to regroup.
Reboot the computer when it isn't behaving.
Save money, every payday, for the future.
Think about what went wrong and why.
Underestimate your importance but not yourself.
Value time with nothing to do.
Walk.
eXamine your motives as well as the other person's.
Yodel to every echo. Echo to every yodel.
Zero in on your next goal.

• • •

Part I, Part 2

AN ELEVEN O'CLOCK SCHOLAR

*(I was in my late fifties when I completed
my BA and began my MFA studies.)*

Favorites from My BA & Master's Classes

Mater Familias

You have to be in Southern California when the moon is full in winter, to see a double lunar halo, so moony white its colors shimmer like you've never seen before—so you *know* it's a sign; and words you swore you'd never speak again shoot off like fireworks in your brain, arcing toward the new man whose arms wreathe you, whose eyes share the silent path of yours toward the moon, like he's never seen it before and maybe he thinks it's a sign—because if any single thing before was different, if your parents hadn't moved from Kansas, you wouldn't be staring up at the Southern California moon with him tonight.

You have to be as moonstruck as you are in love, as scared as you are courageous, as full of hope as you have been full of despair, to marry again, fuse two lives, collide two families; you have to expect joy but tolerate grief, within a chaos of egos compounding like interest—you and your 6- and 8-year-olds, him and his 10-, 12-, 14-, 16-, 18-year-olds, plus future in-laws and offspring, multiplied by the rest of your lives; you have to dispense Band-Aids fast when a family bumps against an unfamiliar family, to heal fast if you want to be Wise Surrogate, not Wicked Stepmother, and to pray your own kids won't get cut on the sharp edges of your divided attention.

You have to be steadfast in your commitment to this man, this family, this life, but when the welcoming root stock resists the grafting limbs, you chastise yourself for betraying your oath never to say those words again, for being foolish/thoughtless/wrong twice—and foggy thoughts of Harry Campbell drift in, and you wonder if you'd slept together in high school like today's guiltless teens, would you have

24

married so foolishly/thoughtlessly/wrongly the first time? . . . and if the new family tree dies, will Harry Campbell be married or single then? . . . but each day you pretend you like the little monsters because you truly believe that someday you will.

You have to be as stubborn as a tick to want to raise the kids of a woman who moved to Hawaii—kids who meet after school in your new oldest daughter's bedroom, chanting your strings of sins—and you have to be convinced you can accomplish fusion single-handed not to carry tales to the new man, who's confounded by the turmoil, distant as that moon; you don't rock the pea-green boat, don't make it worse, don't pack your boys and leave, even though you could float away on your tears—because staying is best for everybody, even if you're the only one who knows it, and the years pass like rolls of film through a camera, and snapshots will fill thirty family albums.

You have to be resilient to be released by a boy of 10 who says, "Hi, need any help with dinner?"—and you rise like a helium balloon, and all the lights look like that halo around the moon, which must have something to do with moisture in the air or in the eye—and you say, "How come you're not in the meeting?" and he says, "They won't let me because I can't think of anything bad to say about you," and you know that's one down, and the rest will follow, and you're ready: you know who drinks nonfat and who drinks whole, who likes mayo and who likes Miracle Whip, who won't use margarine and who won't use butter, and that everyone likes Green Giant Broccoli with Cheese Sauce and flank steak with mushroom gravy and rice, because the way to their hearts is through the open doors of the kitchen.

You have to remind yourself while you're blending the gravy and blending the family that one night you and the new man made love on the beach when the grunion didn't show, and while his fireworks went off, you opened your eyes and saw a meteor shower, and you'd never seen one before, and surely shooting stars were a sign—it's easy to forget that there was a time when you and the new man did only what suited you, the man who is now your husband, who grows apprehensive as voices rise (as all but *his* quite frequently do), who makes evening camp in the bedroom you share, with the door closed and the TV on, and this is how he copes because he's not so sure it's for the best, and his kids knock when they need him because you said "no bad news until after dinner," and you watch *Laugh-In* and *Love Boat* with the kids *not* in there, then glue yourself to him with sex as payment and promise, and you don't learn until years later that he kept a packed suitcase in the trunk of his car, but stayed because he'd made a commitment. You'd find it funny, one day, that he'd have left his kids with you.

You have to think of fun things to do with your kids and the teenagers who've decided you're groovy, and "Let's take tap dancing, modeling, karate" and "Let's have a black-light party, a pool party, a barbecue" and "Let's go to Ensenada, Laguna, Balboa," and "Let's go to Baskin Robbins, Disneyland, the movies, the beach, bowling, ice skating, trampolining, miniature golfing" and "Let's go shopping for something funky," and "Let's go to the mall and count how *few* girls are prettier than you are," and "Let's go to the Mother/Daughter tea, Little League, Olvera Street, China Town, the Planetarium, the Natural History Museum, the doctor, the psychologist" . . . because you're trying so hard to make a family, you've asked your own kids to be patient, to adjust, to blend in, and Dr. Gray says the ones who are "acting out" are the healthy ones, but you feel guilty the rest of your life for reversing your priorities.

You have to do a lot of laundry and smell a lot of shirts' and tops' armpits, because clean clothes and dirty clothes mingle on bedroom floors, and you are afraid to tell your new kids what to do, so you negotiate a compromise: they keep their doors closed and you ignore the jetsam—until you fear strangers will think your kids' armpits smell because no one *cares,* and one day you leave a note in the messiest room, which reads, "[So-and-so], are you in here?" and you think that's so funny, only your heart hurts when your bigger little boy says, "But, Mom, this is *my* house, too" so you grant your own kids the no-nag license; then high school happens, and they want their own socks back from the wash, they do their own laundry, and you don't cross their thresholds again, so as the youngest packs for college, you say, "I forgot there is a carpet in here."

You have to believe you're doing what's best when you keep his kids' secrets, and you don't tell him about taking your middle daughter to the doctor for birth control pills, or about the Dean of Girls showing you your youngest daughter's file of absence excuses that you didn't write but said you did; and thank God the kids believe what their father says about cigarettes being the *worst* thing a kid can do—because when they're ready to rebel, they smoke cigarettes and don't do the *really* worst things a kid can do; but you tell him *your* kids' secrets, and he has a stern chat about stealing Playboy magazine from the 7-Eleven with the littlest boy, the one who calls him "my real Dad"—though the Father Figure has trouble relating to him—and he disposes of your older boy's pot plants from an improvised roof garden without making a big deal about it because—even though this child's the most troublesome—he likes him.

You have to face new problems all the time: you give your second grader Ritalin to control his spontaneous misbehavior because you don't know it will stunt his growth; you worry when the phone rings that it's the school or the police station because your bigger boy has a quick temper and a strong and accurate fist. You have to be fearless to teach kids to drive, fearful they will use drugs, and vigilant that they get their college applications in on time. But it gets easier because kids grow like flowers opening in time-lapse photography, and your first daughter is married, and your second and third go away to college and get married, and the new son who loved you first stays home the longest, and you wish your new kids had bonded better with your own kids, but they're all yours and his, and you've done it—mended two old broken families into one new family and earned the title *mater familias*, and you simply love it.

You have time on your hands with all the kids gone, and things come to a dead stop, so you go to work part time to have more cash for college kids, and at night you drink too much wine while your husband works late to provide for your old age, and in the morning you read the obituaries and wonder why people write letters to dead people, as if dead people read the Los Angeles Times: "Oh, [So-and-so], though it's been ten years, we miss you more each day, but life goes on," and you're reading the letters and the obituaries and wondering . . . if Harry Campbell's mother died, would it be OK to write Harry a note?—and she does die, and you do write a note, and he doesn't answer.

You have to bleed monthly, then you bleed relentlessly, until all you have the energy to do is bleed and make more blood and drift into a bloody depression, and you cry as much as you cried in fifteen years and you don't even consider that it could be declining hormones, not turning 45 that makes the rest of your life a big gift box you're afraid to open for fear it's as empty of accomplishments as the first part, when you didn't fulfill the dreams you or your mother had for you, because of sex and moons and what's best for everybody, and thank God for counseling, and hysterectomies, and Premarin—the Father Figure becomes the new man again, you can have loud sex again, and you buy a 46-inch TV, reclaim the family room, and call it *the den*.

You have to be Grandma-and-Grandpa, and when the new man retires you make your life about flying to visit the kids who've rooted like vines, far away from the mother plant, and you're ecstatic when your oldest granddaughter gets married, and all your kids are together in your house for the first time in more than ten years—but stirred-up dust combusts, and the two daughters who aren't the mother of the bride (who's become your best friend) tell you it's time you get a life, that one big happy family is your fantasy, not theirs, and, besides, you did everything wrong when they were growing up; and thirty tiers of your life implode like an old Las Vegas hotel, your cooking can't open the closed doors, you can't reach those limbs on the family tree, and you mourn; but the moon beams on a new life, you stop crying, and you consider posting a notice in the obits: "We miss you, you so-and-so's, but life goes on."

You have to weep moony tears when your mother, who is losing her memory but remembers the old days, says "I'm proud of you, sweetie. You raised those kids like they were your own, and they all turned out so fine," and you wonder why she couldn't have said she was proud of you sooner, or for *anything* else, but you're glad she's proud of you, and so are you, and if you lose your memory, the photos will remind you it wasn't a fantasy, and you're almost 60 and the gift box with the second half in it is full of good stuff and bad stuff like the first box—and you never tire of speaking those words, and the new man says it was all for the best, and you thank the Southern California moon and your lucky stars that were, indeed, the signs.

• • •

Confronting My Dragons

"Everything I've let go has claw marks on it."
- Anne Lamott

I am afraid of lizards, and some other things. There was a time when those little reptiles kept breaching the boundaries of our new house, scaring the heck out of me. Soon, any movement seen from the corner of my eye startled me. I imagined that any lizard left uncaught would soon give birth out of sight. Successive generations, countless belly crawlers set to terrorize me, would claim my walls, my furnishings, my clothing.

Always on drop-everything alert, my husband Lee tracked each invader before its due date, returned it to its natural habitat, boarded up each vent beneath cupboards, behind sinks, beyond my sight. Soon another lizard—or the same one?—would gain access. One entered by way of the light fixture in our bathroom, rattling the plastic filter that diffuses the fluorescence that attracted him. My hero lifted the panel and whisked the intruder outside.

I'd long suspected that lizards—and other fearsome creatures—live within my walls, but while they stayed beneath the surface, they didn't bother me. In our last house, the white paint on the wood molding around the pantry doorway was but a deceptive shell, hiding the devastation termites had worked beneath the surface. We are vulnerable to so many predators.

I'd never had to defend my territory myself until a day when I was home alone. Claiming my carpeted staircase as his own, doing push-ups midway up, and challenging me with a slow blink of his eye, was the symbol of the terrors of my life, a big grey lizard. Okay, maybe he wasn't so big. But I knew what he was thinking: Take one step closer and I'll run up your leg and lay eggs in your hair. My body froze while my reptilian

brain synchronized my heart to the RPM's of a race car, sent
vibrations to my large muscles, percolated fluids through
their channels. Fight or flight? I raised my eyes, away from
his sideways, one-eyed stare, beseeching heaven for strength
in adversity. I received help in the form of a recollection.

When I was about 16, I'd come home from a date to
find a fuzzy brown moth, a specimen of the genus *largeus
disgustingus* (meaning, don't take one step closer) napping
on my white chenille bedspread. My mother always awakened
when I came home, and I went to her bedroom and whispered
my plight. "I can't get into bed. If I disturb it, it will flit at me
all night long and get moth fuzz on me!" Although fearless
herself, my mother never ridiculed my fears. She told me to
get out the Electolux, put the long metal wand on, and suck
up the moth. That worked. And I stuffed a pair of bobby socks
into the end of the hose so the bat-like thing couldn't escape.

The message of that memory was clear. The angels, the
Universal Mind, God himself—or maybe my mother, by
telepathy—sanctioned the same solution to get rid of the
lizard. I contemplated the prehistoric relic, who blinked at me
at eye level. I gauged that he would neither mount nor
descend the stairs before I could return, and I backed away.
From the closet where we store the accessories for the central
vacuum system, I retrieved the necessities. More quietly than
with that old Electrolux, I sucked up my enemy. For a good
long time, I let the system run. And, in case he'd gotten stuck
in the hose, I inserted one end of it into the other, like that
ringéd snake.

My heart still rampaging in my ears, a dire thought
entered my mind. Was it possible the lizard had lived through
his ordeal and even now was slithering his way back through
the system, into the house, seeking revenge? I dialed my
critter-savvy brother-in-law. He wasn't home, but my sister
did her best to calm me. I followed her advice and called the
vacuum repair store. The man said I had to get the little

dragon out of the tank or it might eat the liner, ruin the filter, and burn out the motor, which would be quite costly.

I couldn't possibly liberate the lizard from the receptacle tank in the garage, and it would be hours before Lee got back. How long would it take an angry lizard to destroy a central vacuum system? I turned to my neighbor Alan for help. "That's not my department," he said. "Those things give me the creeps." A kindred soul, but no help.

Alan's wife Linda agreed to retrieve the lizard. If Linda's afraid of anything, it isn't an animal. She empathizes with them all. I've seen her carry an ant from her kitchen to her backyard and tame a snarling racoon to relocate it miles up-creek. Linda just reached into the dust and with her bare hand pulled out that unnatural beast. He ran home like a lizard out of hell when Linda set him down on the grass.

Now Linda looks at me from only one side of her face, and it's clear she hasn't forgiven me for traumatizing the lizard. I'd never tell her that, when I saw a mouse in my kitchen, I asked Lee to set out traps and poison.

I don't know why I have these unreasonable fears, why I can't let go of them. Maybe because someone always rescues me before I find out what would happen if the things that belong outside, beneath the surface, beyond my awareness, touched me. Having fears isn't something a person outgrows, and new terrors can sink their claws in the elemental brain.

Now I fear a different invader that I *know* could surely touch me, could make a nest, could increase and multiply. I *know* what would happen. The new fear is *reasonable*. My mother not only can't rescue me, if I have it, she implanted me with it. There is no preventive, no protection, no poison.

For twenty years, I've watched my mother, the Alexandrian Library of family history, disappearing, her knowledge evaporating—a life-sized ice sculpture rounding to a smooth, unrecognizable form. My mother still knows who I am. But I don't know who *she* is.

The only fear I remember my mom expressing was that she'd be "a financial burden to her children" in her later years. She prepared against that fear by working to save the money to provide for her independence. Not long after she retired, she began to show symptoms of a failing memory. She complained that no one told her about the bridge luncheon her friends said she forgot. We discovered theater tickets we'd given her in her medicine chest, long past the date of the performance, when she was supposed to treat a friend. And other symptoms, lots of other symptoms.

After our father died, my sister and I helped Mother move into her three-room "senior living apartment," where others would cook and clean for her. We crowded in as much of her furniture, what-nots, and photographs as would fit. Now we don't want to replace the collapsing couch, the scratched tables, the dust-dinged lamp shades. We don't want to remove anything familiar from the nest we made for her when she was 80 and still like our mother. At 91, she is further reduced by physical infirmities. While private care-givers can bathe her, dress her, change her, they cannot attend to her worst affliction. The vacuum of senile dementia sucks away her memories.

Every week or so, Lee and I visit my mother, this hollowing shell, pale as soapstone. Sometimes she asks the same question over and over, and I answer it over and over. Sometimes I must struggle to think of things to say, as if to a stranger. I repeat the family news several times, each time rephrasing it, as though the right combination of words will navigate the strangulated arteries of her brain, penetrate her basal ganglia where plaques and tangles form at will, and slip a new image into the muddled album there.

On a recent visit, I scanned her apartment for topics. My sister and I have arranged with the woman who does her hair to bring her fresh-cut flowers each week. "The carnations are so pretty," I said, wondering whether she notices flowers any more.

"Oh, I picked those up at that little shop in the Farmer's Market this morning. I thought they were cheery," she told us. I was surprised and glad that a pleasant memory echoed for her—however untimely. I said yes, they look very fresh. Then she said, "Daddy can't get the roses to grow anymore. Shouldn't he be coming to pick me up in a little while?"

"And where will you be going then?" I asked. (My sister and I are protective of the precarious balance of her happiness and go along with whatever our mother says. She becomes distressed if confronted with her inability to remember.)

"Well, home of course. I can't sit around here all day!" Home, the house my parents shared for thirty years, which she hasn't seen for over a decade. I have no idea where she thinks she is if this apartment, with her furnishings, is not her home. "Yes, well, we have to be on our way, too," I said.

"Better get on the road ahead of the traffic." She says this each time Lee and I leave. I wonder why, when she can access so little conversational matter, she can think to speak of traffic. Somewhere a healthy blood vessel nourishes memories in her brain of driving children around, commuting to work, running errands, visiting her family.

Lee kissed my mother on the forehead, wished her a happy day. "Good-bye. Thanks for coming," my mother said to him. Lee waited a few steps away while I said "I love you, Mom," and kissed her on same waxy spot. "I love you too, sweetie," she said. "Be sure and say hello to Lee for me." And then we were gone, and she didn't know we'd been there.

I think of our father's slide shows, images of family vacations, new houses, growing grandchildren. Packed with our memories, the slide carousel clicked as it fed the projector each different image to illuminate the silvery screen. And as the carousel clicked, the screen went black for a moment, like the slow blink of that lizard's eye, and what was there before the blink . . . is gone after the blink.

Will traffic be my mother's last image before the show is over and the screen stays dark?

If we are a compilation of our memories, what are we when we have no memory? What is it that survives? A painted shell, hollowed by hidden predators? Are my memory-hitches and mental-glitches benign aging, or indications of a mind disintegrating? *Will I be just like her? Will my sons be just like me?*

Every once in a while, I get a picture in my mind of that lizard flying through the vacuum ducts in the walls, around blind corners, toward the noisy unknown. I imagine him fanning out the pointy toes of all four feet, trying to get a grip on the edges as he is sucked through the dark, deafened with fear. He was probably more frightened than I'll *ever* be.

But when thoughts of the great unknown scare me, I see myself as that lizard, grasping at the now, the present, today. My mother went into the darkness, fearless, unsuspecting, without a fight. I prepare like ants for a long winter, exercise my intellect as if it's a muscle that can clench and defend me, scratch signs to be read by those who come behind me.

When my turn is over and I've flown through the vacuum to who knows where, like the lizard in Linda's hand I'll welcome the terrain I'm set upon. It's what might happen between then and now that scares me.

• • •

AFTER STORY
Two of my mother's siblings also had dementia. I was so concerned about myself I had my memory tested at the Senior Services Center of UC Irvine Hospital. When they said that I showed no signs of memory failure or potential dementia, I cried. Then, I *totally* stopped worrying about anything I might have forgotten.

The next story is very special to me. My husband Lee and I found the Taj Mahal to be the grandest sight we ever visited on our travels. This story fulfilled a unique writing requirement.

See if you can determine what it was.

The Moon of the North Realm

How pale she looks, as if she paid for this sweet gift with her last drop of blood.

"Swear, my Shah, that when I'm gone, yet shall I be here with you. No wife will share your bed nor wrench me from your heart."

The Shah combs his wife's sweat-curled hair. *It is true what the scribe writes of her, he thought: The moon hides its face in shame when it sees Mum Taz.* "You must rest, my love. Feed our son while you can. Your sweet cream is part of me, and your sweet milk will make you part of him."

"But swear it first, or I shall not rest—not in this life, not in the next," she cries.

"I do swear, on the great Khan! Of all my wives, you are the one who owns my heart. When you die, I shall have no need of it."

Mum Taz' fist lets go the Shah's arm, and her small frame sinks back on her bed, soft with the down of scores of geese. "But for our heirs you must keep heart! Of ten and four, half have gone to God. Give our love to the rest, all but the son who kills me now. He cried in my womb, my Shah! Like a knife he slit me, and he will be the end of you."

The Shah can't think of a son born bent while he tends his wife at the door of death.

"It is the end of you that will be the end of me. When you leave this earth, no sight on it will cheer me."

"Then build my tomb like no tomb at all—with no peer as our love has no peer, so grand that you can't help but see it, so light that it lifts your soul till God lifts you up to me!"

"Name what you want, and so shall it be."

Mum Taz shuts her eyes. "Tell me what you dream, my Shah, and I shall rest as you bid me."

Then the Shah gave birth, and his plan took voice. "I shall build you a shrine more grand than the moon that you dim. I shall shape it of the rock that shines like pearls, carve it to a dome that taunts the skies. In the strong light of day it shall glow as white as the breast of a dove. The set of the sun shall turn it as gold as your warm, silk flesh, and the light of each new dawn shall turn it as pink as the rose in your cheeks. On its walls, I will tell of our love in ore of gold and gems of jade and all the stones most dear to man. I will see it each day I live, thus I will live. Day and night, founts will sing and I will hear your voice. All kith and kin of the earth will come to praise you . . . "

Mum Taz does not hear the rest. The smile that curves her lips is her last gift.

The Shah wept as no man has wept ere or yet. For one week, he did not eat nor did he drink. His hair grew white as the clouds of spring. When at last he came from his tent, he sought the best men of each craft—those who would cut stone, those who would carve wood, those who would trace his words of love. He set to work ten men times ten, times ten, times ten, times two, for twice ten years plus two. And when they laid their tools down, there stood The Taj.

The Shah could see the shrine through the air arch in his cell in the Red Fort, where he spent his last eight years of life. Mum Taz' son held the key.

• • •

BACKSTORY:

"The Moon of the North Realm" creatively manipulates what is known about Shah Jehan Mahal and his wife Mum Taz. While Mum Taz died as a result of childbirth, the Shah was not with her. Also, their son indeed did depose and incarcerate the Shah, but although Mum Taz' died in childbirth, her last child was a daughter. Other facts in the story are true to available information.

Professor's Instruction:
Write a story using words of only one syllable.
Did you guess?

Memory Poem

Rosary—1951

I didn't want piano lessons anymore.
If Miss O'Grady moved away, or we went to Timbuktu,
That would've been OK with me, but Miss O'Grady died.
Here we are—the whole church full.
My mother, big and solid,
Miss O'Grady way up front in a great big shining box,
Gleaming like the tabernacle, like the monstrance sun—
Monsignor, big as the altar, whistles "full of grace,
    blessed is, Jesus."
       (We answer him a hundred and fifty times . . .)

In my new red hooded raincoat, I look twelve already.
Mother dreamed I'd play at assemblies just like Linda Burns.
But I and Miss O'Grady knew I never would.
       (All fifteen mysteries—sorrowful, joyful, glorious . . .)

You can smell the gentlemen's wet wool suits,
The wet black straw of women's hats, and flowers.
Purple and white stock, even fresh, smell like rotten-flower
    water.
I've never been to a Rosary for the Dead.
You can't see the stained glass saints at night.
    *(Glory Be and Our Father come between each
decade . . .)*

Droning voices makes me sleepy.
Mother presses her arm into mine.
My thumbnail feeds each aqua bead into my fist,
The circle endless till the last amen.
       (Over at last. Let's go. No . . .)

Monsignor flaps his lacy wings, holy-waters
Miss O'Grady's green-and-white carnation blanket.
Mutters Latin syllables, all except
ROSEANNA O'GRADY, ROSEANNA O'GRADY.
Swings the smoking censor, down-up-up, down-up-up—
    gold chains clink in threes.
The heavy incense smell can lift a ghost to heaven.
    (Over at last. Let's go. No . . .)

Dies Irae on the organ. Churches do not have pianos.
Men in black open up Miss O'Grady's splendid box.
People line up, like for Communion.
I don't want to go. Mother grips my upper arm.
We sway up the aisle, stop a moment.
I see a life-sized, cradled doll—red wig, eyes that close,
Painted face that's old, dry, dead—
Not like the lifeless shining statues looking down.
What a mean thing to do, to spy on dead old Miss O'Grady!
Mother hands me Kleenex. But I don't cry, I shudder.
    (I'll never let them open up my box.)

Epilog—1985

When my dear friend Marilyn died a sad and early death,
I sat for a while by her casket, glad to be able to say goodbye.
And I changed my mind.
    (It's over at last. Let her go.)

• • •

Irony

Ode to Those
Who Died Doing What They Loved to Do

Parents push a child who flies:
Breaks a record, falls from skies.

Age-repellers having tucks,
rib removals, life-o-sucks.

Celeb skiers buy the ranch
Hit by tree or avalanche.

Mountain climbers on the slopes
Frozen to their safety ropes.

Race car drivers in their cars,
Alcoholics in their bars,
Dopers shooting up their necks,
Viagra-takers having sex.

What they loved, they lived to do.
And they didn't have a clue
What they loved they'd die for, too.

• • •

Parody

Poe-M

Edgar Allen's fate was shocking!
To my room, I was a-walking,
When I heard my neighbor squawking
Just inside his garret door.
Imitating bird-ish cooing
Is what caused his sad undoing,
And I rushed to phone, a-strewing
Yellow Pages on my floor.
"Dr. Savem? Please come quickly
For my neighbor is quite sickly,
And I fear he's wacky-wickly—
Hooting, raving, 'Nevermore.'"
Dr. Savem and his wagon
Came. He poured a measured flagon
Down that literary dragon
And took him to his store.
Soon the padded room was locking,
Next day's headlines, sadly mocking,
"Poet Has Electro-shocking:
May See Daylight Nevermore!"
Now I suffer, lonely, guilty,
weeping shame into my quilty.
Alas, too late! The milk is spilty,
And a raven's at my door.

• • •

Part II, Part 1

PREVIOUSLY PUBLISHED

(Not likely you've read them before)

From *Coast Magazine*

The following story represents the first "income" I received for my writing. Shortly after Lee and I moved to Newport Beach, I entered a contest in *Coast Magazine,* an Orange County, CA, publication.

The subject of the essay was "My First Car," and the winner would receive an epoxy garage floor.

"Hmm. We'd like that," I thought. "And I have so much to say about my '59 Chevy!"

And lo and behold, I won the epoxy garage floor!

It reminds me daily that I can write.

From *Coast Magazine*, October 2002

My First Car

I never had my own car when I was in school. On rare occasions, I was allowed to drive the family Oldsmobile. Otherwise, I depended on girlfriends or boyfriends to get me where the gang was going.

While I was married, we made do with one car. One car at a time, that is. My husband liked the newest and the oddest.

The one decorated with "Just Married" was a 1960 Ford Falcon. It had a stick shift, and the only time I drove it was when my husband had an appendectomy. I navigated the back streets of Los Angeles to visit him in the hospital. He risked splitting his stitches to drive us home—a lesser risk, he felt. I wasn't skilled in stick-shifting, and the Falcon was more like a jack rabbit under my control.

That was the last time I drove for over five years. I was a stay-at-home mom to the nth degree. Either my husband drove me, or I handled what errands I could on foot with a baby stroller.

The last car we owned was a '64 VW Beetle, teal blue. He got the car, and I got the furniture and the kids.

I was 26 years old when I bought my first car, in January of 1966. My work skills were five years' rusty, and the only place that would hire me paid minimum wage. What I could afford, for monthly car payments of $50, bought me a white '59 four-door Chevy with automatic transmission—the model with the wide cat's-eye tail fins. A boat of a car. A battered and rejected, out-of-style, almost-embarrassment of a boat that rescued me for my first voyages as a woman on my own.

Water metaphors seem suitable. I had no garage to protect the Chevy, and its back doors and back floor filled with water when it rained. On right- and left-hand turns, it sloshed like a washing machine. Its turn signals didn't work unless you held the lever on. Every month or so it needed something replaced, from the starter to the brakes. But for my sons and me, it was a dreamboat. For the first time in our lives, we could float along wherever we wanted, whenever we wanted.

I filled the tank with 25-cents-a-gallon gas, and off we cruised to the beach, to the zoo, to the grandparents', and mercifully even to the market. No more walking to the store for my two little boys and me, buying our food daily, a stroller-full at a time! In fact, no more walking. I gained 15 pounds after that, but I told myself I looked better rounded out a bit, and all that water in the doors? It just gave me extra buoyancy.

Or maybe the buoyancy I felt back then was the freedom that came with my '59 Chevy.

• • •

From *A Community of Voices*

The next five stories were published in *A Community of Voices,* compiled and edited by Grace Rachow. Each annual edition is an anthology of submissions from staff and students of the Santa Barbara Writer's Conference. Each edition of *A Community of Voices* has a different name and theme.

48

From "Winging It With Words" - 1997

Fear of Falling

Jill thought it had gone all right. The cousins played well together. Ted had matched beers with her brother-in-law all afternoon. He'd bull-shitted with her brother around the barbecue and smoked an after-dinner cigar with her father. No one knew. Of course, her mother commented on Jill's weight loss, but her sister pretended to be jealous of it. No one had guessed. Just a normal Mother's Day.

As she finished putting away the serving dishes, Jill could hear her three- and four-year-old sons giggling and splashing in the tub in the bathroom on the other side of the thin kitchen wall. In the tiny house she and Ted had bought six months ago, she could even hear Ted hang up the phone in the living room.

He was holding the car keys when he spoke to her. "I'm going out," he said.

She saw him watching her face as her mind cycled through the possibilities. *Oh, please be going out to get milk. You know we ran out of milk today. Or be meeting Mike for a drink. That would be OK, too.*

"Where are you going," she asked.

"I'm going to Leah's. I'll be back later."

"Please don't do this. Please don't go to her today!" The shivering started, and she turned on the floor heater as she passed through the living room to check on the boys.

"It was your idea to share me. That was the deal. We stay together, and I can see Leah."

"You are in dick heaven, aren't you. Screwing either of us whenever you want!" Her teeth chattered as she spoke. "Don't you care about my feelings at all? How could you leave me on Mother's Day?"

"Another volley of guilt? Religion, marriage vows, and now motherhood. I don't give a rat's ass. We can go on fooling your family if that's what you want, but stop fooling yourself."

"I thought it would go away. I thought if you could have her with my knowledge, you would lose interest. I thought . . . if I could just hang in there, it would run its course."

The little that Jill had eaten for dinner began to roil in her stomach.

"Well, that remains to be seen. I'm going now. Don't wait up."

"No! Not this time! If you go, I'll move all your stuff onto the porch, and it's over. I'll bolt the doors. You want Leah? You can live with Leah." It scared Jill that she'd said that.

"You're whistling in the dark. You won't throw me out. You're holding on so tight your knuckles are white. You don't know how to be alone. Hey, I'll pick up some milk on the way home." And he left.

Jill toweled off her children, helped them with their pajamas, and tucked them in bed. "Sweet dreams," she said and closed their bedroom door.

Then she closed the bathroom door and knelt down by the toilet and threw up. For the next few hours, she alternated between crying in their bed, shivering next to the heater, and vomiting. All the while, she heard Ted's voice.

Oh, baby, I love you so much. I can't wait for you to finish college. Let's get married now. Quit school and get a job . . .

Oh, baby, I love you so much. Hey, how much money have you got? My boss thinks I stole something, and he's going to report me if I don't give him the money. No, of course I didn't. It's just not worth the hassle . . .

I'm going out for a drink with Mike and Judy. No, you can't come. You're not 21, and I'm not going to spend good money for you to drink sodas . . .

What are you complaining about? You knew I was selfish when you married me . . .

It's my day off, and I'm playing golf . . .

I didn't buy you an anniversary (birthday, Valentine's, etc.) gift because I didn't have enough money to get you something as good as you deserve . . .

So what if are seven months' pregnant. You have to look for work or you can't collect unemployment . . .

Don't wait up. I'm going to help Mike bartend after work . . .

Don't wait dinner. I may stop for a drink on my way home.

Yes, there is another woman. What are you going to do about it? I just married you to have kids and avoid the draft. They'll send women and children to Vietnam before they'll send me!

I can't support two households! And who will hire you? You don't have any skills. Who'd want you? Divorcees with kids are a dime a dozen. A dime a dozen. A dime a dozen.

The electric blanket, turned up to nine, hadn't warmed her. Jill dried her eyes and stood by the heater. *I could blow out the pilot light,* she thought, and again her mouth filled with the water of warning.

When all that was left to vomit was bile, Jill lay on the cold bathroom floor exhausted. As if she were looking at some pitiful stranger, she asked herself, *How could being alone possibly be worse than this?*

Returning to the bedroom, she opened Ted's side of the closet: suits, slacks, shirts—she'd never have to iron those shirts again—ties, belts, wingtip shoes. She carried them all to the small front porch. She carried out each of his dresser drawers and dumped alpaca sweaters and Jockey shorts atop the pile. She dropped his unused wedding ring into the wastebasket. His jewelry box, golf tees, match books, Playboy magazines— everything that was special to him, everything in the small house that would remind her of him—she pushed it into the dark.

Finally, balanced against the porch railing, went the shadow box Ted had made, in which he displayed his British toy soldiers, out of the reach of his sons.

Jill bolted the doors and waited in the dark living room. She heard Ted's car come, noises on the porch stop, and the car drive away.

Then she went to bed, and dreamed of flying.

In the morning, all of Ted's belongings were gone, a half gallon of homogenized milk sat in the brimming sunlight, and Jill was happy with the Mother's Day gift she had given herself.

• • •

From "Horsing Around" - 1998

Kansas, 1945

"Don't slam the screen door!" Mother shouts.

It is just before my bedtime on a Saturday in late summer. I am almost six years old. Fat red tomatoes hang waiting as a snack for my sister and brother and me in the Victory Garden my father planted when he couldn't go to the war. My brother is carrying the salt shaker as we walk past the baby tomato plants that line the path between the garden and the house. Daddy says they grew from the seeds our teeth squirted out early in the summer.

I like to eat the vegetables in Daddy's garden—small orange carrots you just rub the dirt off of, blue-green asparagus spears, snap peas, and crunchy string beans. Once they get in Mother's kitchen, she cooks them till they're gray.

But tonight Evie and Walter and I got melted cheese sandwiches and raw green pepper strips. Tonight Mother and Daddy are going to dinner with friends, and Evie and Walter will babysit me. They are big kids. My brother will start at Wyandotte High School in one month. Evie will be in eighth grade at St. Peter's Grammar School, and I'll be in first grade there. I can't wait to be one of the big kids.

Evie and I lean far over the grass so we will not get tomato squirts on our sundresses. They are alike except for the size. Aunt Babe, who has only boys for children, made them for us. They have ruffles over our shoulders, like butterfly wings, and bows in the back.

Walter holds a fat tomato far in front of him and squeezes it so it will get us messy, but the insides shoot up in the air. Evie laughs, but I just keep away from Walter. My brother doesn't like me. He goes "Boo!" at me from around corners and grabs my ankles from behind the cellar stairs. My sister likes me. She lets me hang around her and her friends.

"Finish that up and come inside, Beth," Mother calls. I hate going to bed when it's still light out, and it will be light for a long time.

Mother always tucks me into bed before she goes out—even when it's hot and sticky like today, only now with just the sheet. I wonder if she will still do this when I am eight. I especially hate being in bed when Evie and Walter are laughing at something on the radio. They'll make popcorn and I'll smell it, and I'll hear ice jingling in their glasses of grape juice. I am feeling very sorry for myself until Mother reminds me about the ice cream social at the church tomorrow.

Mother and Daddy have been gone for not too long when Evie shakes my shoulder. I am not asleep. I am facing the wall singing "Dance with the Dolly with the Hole in her Stocking" to my doll Regina.

"You can get up," Evie says. Walter's going to play a trick outside. We don't want to leave you alone, so you can come with us."

"Honest? I get to come, too?" I am moving quickly to put on my sundress before Evie changes her mind. *I get to go with the big kids!*

"No, put on your denims," Evie says. "We're going to be climbing Miss Haver's pear tree. Hurry up! Walter is in the garage getting some string or something. We'll meet him at the corner."

Evie has her denims on, too, and I'm so excited about going on an adventure with the big kids that I think I should go tinkle even though I tinkled before I went to bed, but Evie is pulling my hand and I am sweating when we get to the corner. When you rush in the summer, your shirt sticks to you and you never dry off.

Walter is already in the neighbor's big old pear tree, which sits on a little slope at the corner of Miss Haver's property.

Evie boosts me from behind and Walter pulls me up onto a thick branch. I sit on it like it's a horse. I can see the whole corner where the road turns. It's not a real corner with four streets but a big bend in the road, and the branches of the pear tree hang out over it.

"Hurry up, fishbait! And don't make any noise," my brother says as I scooch toward the trunk so I can hold on. He always calls me not nice names, but I do exactly what he says so he doesn't send me home with Evie. She shinnies up the tree like a monkey-on-a-stick I got at the Halloween carnival. She's as good at boy things as Walter is, and almost as big.

Walter moves toward the end of his branch, and I'm surprised to see that another boy with his back to me is out there with him. "Evie, who is that?"

"That's not real. It's a dummy," Evie says. "Walter stuffed his old clothes with newspapers. Now hush, or he'll get cross."

I put my finger across my lips to show I understand. I recognize the clothes now—Walter's old brown wash pants that are even too short for Evie, and his red flannel shirt. A black stocking cap from last winter is stretched low over the dummy's paper-bag head. It's got gloves for hands and galoshes for feet.

My brother holds a coil of heavy yellow twine in one hand. The twine is wrapped around the chest of the dummy.

"This is Howard," Walter whispers. He has named the dummy after our mother's cousin. Walter likes to make fun of Howard by walking in a sissy way and moving his lips in little puckers when he talks. Cousin Howard is always nice to me, but I giggle so Walter will think I'm a good sport.

My sister has her arm around me, and I twist around so I can put my lips close to her ear. "What are we waiting for?"

"He said he wants to scare his buddies when they come by," Evie says. "We're waiting for them."

"How does he know they'll come?" I ask.

"I don't know, silly!"

I get restless waiting for things to happen. Evie sits patiently and I try to imitate her.

Sometimes the neighbor lady's pear tree grows hard sweet pears that smell really good, called Winter Nellis. Today the tree is covered with just leaves, and you'd have to know we're up here to see us. I bet even Miss Haver doesn't know we're up here in her tree. Her house is pretty far from the street. Mother says this used to be all farm land, and the house on the corner is the original old farmhouse and the lady is the farmer's niece.

Miss Haver has a hairy black spot on her cheek, which is probably why she never got married. Sometimes on summer evenings she comes over to our porch and drinks iced tea and listens to the baseball game with Mother and Daddy. I stop catching fireflies in my Mason jar and sit on the steps and pretend to listen to the big people, but I'm really looking at the neighbor lady's black spot. It's shaped like a big peanut shell. I like to sit around with the grownups, but when my mother notices me, she remembers it's time for me to go to bed. That's my least favorite time of day.

This is my favorite time of day, when the sky is gold, and my shadow gets tall and skinny, and a few crickets start to chirrup. The breeze is blowing just enough to make my sweat feel cool, and I am happy.

I hear a car coming toward us, but as it comes into view, I don't recognize it. The car will pass right under my brother and Harold. I get a funny feeling between my chest and my tummy and I look at my brother. He has used the twine to lower the dummy to where its feet stick out of the leaves and I see him let go of the circle of twine and I know something bad is going to happen, and the dummy disappears and the brakes screech and my brother shouts "Hah! Hah! Hah!" and my sister takes a huge breath and her eyes look like they'll fall out and she scrambles down the tree telling me to hurry hurry and I fall part way and bump my head, and Evie grabs me under the arms and half drags me across the neighbor's backyard and into our house, and she lets the screen door slam.

I hide between the green legs of the stove while I catch my breath. I am scared and very mad at my brother.

I can hear Walter's steps on the front porch.

"There's a man running after him," my sister shrieks. "What are we going to do? What if he comes in the house, and, and, and . . ."

I crawl into the dining room where I can see everything through the cream-colored lace cloth that covers Mother's dining room table.

Walter barges in the front door like he's playing tag and our front rug is Safety or King's X. He just stands with his back to the wall beside the door. The man stops outside the screen. He's very polite, like he's going to try to sell my sister Fuller brushes, but his face is red, and I can tell he's holding back how mad he is.

"Is your mother at home, little girl?" he asks my sister.

"No, sir," my sister says. Her voice is quavery and I know she wants to run into our bedroom and cry, but she's being brave, like she's the lady of the house.

"Is your father home then?" The man's chest is heaving, big and little, like the accordion cousin Harold plays Polish songs on. The man seems almost as tall and as wide as the doorway.

"No, sir," Evie says again. "Our parents are out for the evening."

"Your brother just did a very dangerous thing," the man says. His voice is spooky, like Father O'Reilly's when he talks about sin.

We'd done a sin. I just don't know what kind of sin.

"You two gave me quite a fright. I could have had a heart attack."

Oh, no! We'd almost committed murder!

"Yes, sir. Well, I mean it was an accident. The dummy slipped out of his hands. I know that's what happened. My brother told me we were going to play a trick on his friends."

Evie looks at Walter and I can see his face. He sticks his tongue out at her and puts his thumbs in his ears and wiggles his fingers. My sister narrows her eyes at him, and I know that means she is madder than scared now.

The man shrinks down to a normal size. His voice stops sending off sparks, and he speaks nicer to my sister. "I shall have to change my tire. I smashed into the curb to avoid hitting what I thought was someone falling out of a tree. My tire is ripped open. Do you suppose your brother might help me change it?"

Quick as a lizard's tongue, my sister's hand shoots out and catches my brother's upper arm. "I'm sure he'd be glad to help you, sir. He's right here. I'm sure he's sorry he caused you the trouble." Evie jerks my brother so hard he staggers into the doorway.

"Yes, sir. I'm very sorry I caused you the trouble. I didn't mean to drop the dummy. It just got away from me. My friends, I meant to trick my friends with it. They'll be coming by in a little while. I-I-I'll be glad to help you change your tire, sir," Walter says.

The man takes Walter by the ear to lead him to the corner. "Tell your parents that I will return tomorrow to have a chat with them about this, little girl."

"Yes, sir," Evie says.

Evie knows where to find me. She lifts the tablecloth and joins me in my cave. "Are you all right? Did you hurt yourself bad?"

Now that it's over, I start crying. I know it doesn't have anything to do with the little bump on the back of my head. Evie gets an ice cube wrapped in the end of the flour sack we use to dry the dishes, and she presses it against the bump. Then she takes a handkerchief from her pocket and wipes my eyes and makes me blow my nose. Mother taught her to always have a hanky in her pocket.

"I'd better get you to bed," she says. "And don't tell Mother or Daddy about this. We won't tell them you were there. Better to get in trouble for leaving you alone in the house than for including you in a dumb thing like that. When Walter gets back, I'm going to give him a licking—even if I get pounded myself."

My sister puts me to bed, but I sneak back under the dining room table. When Walter gets back, she whops him on the leg with Mother's big donut spatula. I know that stings because Mother uses it on my fanny when I'm naughty. I can see that Walter's been crying even before Evie hit him. He is sniffling, and there are snotty spots on his cheeks, smeared with the black dirt from the tires. Harold crumples to the floor.

"Stop it!" Walter says. "Knock it off, you dumb girl. Did you think I was going to sit in a tree and hope my friends happened by?"

Evie whops him again. "If you're so smart, how come you're the one who's crying?"

"I'm not crying and I'll pound you if you tell anybody I was crying. I'll pound you if you ever tell anyone about this. Ever. Now cut it out."

But Evie doesn't cut it out. She swats him again. "You are so dumb. You could've killed that man, and you almost got your little sister killed falling out of that tree. Mother's going to wring your neck. She'll give you such a licking you won't be able to sit down for a week."

"I don't think she'll find out." Walter wipes his nose on the arm of his shirt, not even dodging another of Evie's swoops at him with the spatula. I'm surprised he lets her hit him, but if he hits her back, I am going to bite him if I can. It is quiet all of a sudden.

"And why not? The man said he'd be back. He was pretty mad." Evie holds the spatula in one hand while she props her elbow in the other I have seen our mother do this.

"He said he has to be in Chicago Monday. We'll be at church and then at the ice cream social tomorrow. If I'm lucky, he'll either come when we're not here, or he won't come at all. He made me change his damn tire. And he walloped me good, for gosh sakes. Isn't that enough? I was only horsing around."

It doesn't sound like enough to me, but maybe if Evie whopped him a couple more times . . . and if Walter would go to Confession about almost murdering the man, and for cussing, too. I decide it's time to sneak back to bed. I'm already thinking about the ice cream social.

The next morning, Walter and Evie and I are very good. We eat our fried cornmeal mush and don't spill syrup on the tablecloth, and we clear our dishes without being told. Walter's galoshes are in the mud room, so Walter must've taken Harold apart after I went to sleep and hid the evidence of our sin.

Things are like they usually are on a Sunday morning. Evie and Walter are reading the funny papers on their stomachs on the floor, waiting till it's time to go to church.

Daddy won't notice Walter used his twine because it's Daddy's indoors day when he reads the big newspaper. That's lucky because when Mother washes the kitchen floor tomorrow, she will have plenty of want ads for us to walk on while it dries, and she won't miss the newspapers that were Harold's stuffings.

Like she always does before church on Sunday, Mother is curling my hair and telling me to stand still. The electricity in the curling iron broke, so there's just a nubbin on the end of the green handle where Daddy cut off the cord with his pocket knife. Mother heats the metal part in the gas flame of the stove, testing it on toilet paper so it doesn't scorch my hair. I play with the brown-and-gold curly tissue squares while she twirls the shiny grippers, making tight blond columns all around my head. The bump has gone away, but I try not to think about last night in case Mother peeps into my mind.

We went to St. Peter's for Mass and to the ice cream social after. Daddy rode me around on his shoulders like I was flying above the crowd, and the man never came back, even though I expected him every day, until we moved to California.

. • .

From "Hot Dog!" - 1999

Chili Dog Therapy

There's a place in Sherman Oaks called the Wiener Factory where the chili dogs possess restorative powers. Perhaps the Factory (which is not a factory) sits in a mystic center of the Universe, a pocket-sized Sedona. Perhaps the healing attributes emit from the sacred grounds of native tribes that camped along that stretch of El Camino Real now called Ventura Boulevard. A couple miles west, visitors at Los Encinos Historical Park imagine they can smell phantom tortillas frying... until they realize it's just the aroma wafting from El Torito, on the other side of the pond. What matter the cause? I can attest to the occurrence of emotional and physical healing at my hotdog spa.

The Wiener Factory is a dandelion in the area's garden of posh eateries. The psychedelic lean-to looks like a dump, but it bears an A cardboard in one lace-curtained window. The walls of the fist-size indoor eating area, painted French's mustard yellow, are covered with silly one-liners, hand-printed ungrammatically in fat black marker, reflecting the degree of seriousness with which the owner takes life.

The palate purist can obtain a dog at the walk-up window outside and eat it at one of the umbrella-shaded concrete tables. As for me, the full effect takes place inside at a table where someone might join you when it's crowded, which it always is at lunchtime.

I don't recommend deconstructing a heaping chili-cheese dog in your car.

While liquor and chocolate have their places in my life, I'm not a drown-your-sorrows kind of person, nor the kind to eat a pound of See's when faced with frustration. I'm a Leo, and Leos cope.

However, when mildly depressed, or headache-y, I want a Weiner Factory CCMO—a chili cheese-mustard-onion dog. A soft bun hugging a hot crackling dog hidden under savory, drippy chili, topped with onions like silver confetti and cheddar like shredded gold.

That combo pleases all my senses and satisfies my need for something special in a critical moment. Before I master the last bursting mouthful, I feel so-o-o much better.

My reliance upon "dog therapy" began about 25 years ago when my friend Maggie moved to my neck of the San Fernando Valley. For the next 15 years, she and I shared this "cure-inary" oasis. Maybe a half dozen times a year, a call from either of us that started with "poor me" was likely to end with "I'll meet you at the Wiener Factory." When her kid got in trouble. When my kids got in trouble. When her kid said "I hate you." Whey my stepkids said "I hate you." When she got a traffic ticket. When I got a rejection slip. When her husband was being intolerably critical. When my husband was being intolerably perfect. If Maggie had seven kids, too, we might have sapped the therapeutic powers of the Weiner Factory.

It's impossible to know what all we'll have to cope with in life, but it's inevitable that something will come along that a chili dog can't cure. About ten years ago, Maggie began to descend into the cellar of Alzheimer's Disease. At first we met at the Factory and laughed about her undiagnosed tricks of memory. Then one day she got lost trying to find the Weiner Factory, and, too soon, she got lost trying to find the kitchen in her own home.

Even when I eat alone at the Weiner Factory, I have lots of memories for company.

A chili dog with all the trimmings can't ease the loss of a dear friend, but it still has the power to tilt my focus toward all the good stuff in my life. Though I live a fair distance away now, when I need renewing, I still go to the Wiener Factory. Just the other day I went there depressed about the degenerative indignities of aging that my 91-year-old mother experiences. If she were mentally aware of what's going on, I'd have brought her along for a dose of CCMO.

Of course, the Wiener Factory doesn't advertise its chili dogs' ability to lift the heart, strengthen resolve, and remove the weight of the world. It doesn't speak of a possible link to ancient shamans and sacred ground. It makes only one claim, on the faded sign that tops its slanted roof: "We've sold over 4 hot dogs this year."

They'd sold me more than that by February.

• • •

AFTER STORY:
The Weiner Factory is no more. A greedy property owner tore down the old shanty and allowed a new frozen yogurt joint to occupy the spot, but soon the place sat empty and unrented.

I think the Universe wants the Weiner Factory back.

From "When We Were Young—Childhood" - 2000

The Blessing

I was no more than five when I learned about the blessing. That was before the end of World War II, before my family moved to Los Angeles from Kansas City, Kansas. My father was president of the Optimist Club then, and my mother said she belonged to the Spring Cleaning Club, whose activities she promised I would one day enjoy.

Some years my mother started her annual chores while it was still cold outside. She cleaned out the linen closet. She sorted through my brother's bureau drawers, making a pile of his outgrown clothes to give to the church. She packed away my big sister's too-small dresses to save until they would fit me. But some spring cleaning tasks had to wait until the coal dust of our winter's heat had settled.

I remember one spring in particular because it was the first time Mom tried to get me hooked on housework. On a fair and breezy Monday in May, she took down the curtain rods from the four windows in our living room. She stripped off the sheer white panels that had grown limp and sooty as winter drew to an end, bunched together a small dusty-smelling bundle for me, and gathered the rest into her big arms. We carried our airy parcels to the service porch where the green GE machine was already churning White King soap flakes into sudsy water.

Mom circled the curtains around the agitator and poked the ballooning fabric into the scalding water with a bamboo stick my father had fashioned from an old fishing pole. Soon the curtains sloshed in a rolling spiral, turning the water gray as the service porch filled with steam. When the washer had finished, Mom's stick served to feed the tangled curtains from the grimy water through the wringer and into fresh water in one of the stationary tubs. Then Mom swung the wringer arm around and fed the rinsed lot into the other stationary tub where the water was thickened with Argo starch. Finally the curtains slipped from the wringer into the bushel basket, like a continuous ribbon of vanilla taffy.

Waiting in the back yard was a contraption that looked as fragile as a grasshopper but could sting like a hornet—our curtain stretcher. For the past year, it had been confined to the basement, a collapsed bundle of wooden slats studded with nails, prey to spiders and dirt. My father had reassembled the curtain stretcher after church on Sunday. He propped apart its easel-legs and slid the wing nuts along the openings in the overlapping edges of the slats, matching the ruled markings to the curtains' measurements—six feet across and four feet down. Then he hosed off the apparatus to prepare it for Monday's undertaking. The curtain stretcher was a labor-saving device, at least for my mother. Properly stretched curtains could be put right back up, without ironing.

My part of the task was to locate a corner of each curtain, hand it up to Mom, and keep the curtain from dragging on the ground as she shook it free of the flattened pack. Every starchy curtain crackled as it unfurled, reclaiming its length and breadth from the compressing of the wringer.

Mother secured the top corners of the curtain on the stretcher. Then, with her big thumbs, she pressed the edges of the curtain against every fourth little sharp spike, making shallow scallops. Every once in a while, the rhythm of the task failed her by a fraction of an inch, and she cried out, "Ouch!" I shuddered and wondered how she could complete the task without rimming the curtains with spots of blood. But my mother barely paused. She squeezed her pricked thumb, licked away the red dot, and continued until all of the damp curtains lay one atop the other, stretched taut.

Hours later, the breeze and the sun had done their part. The nails pinged as Mom removed the stuck-together curtains, as if one, from the stretcher. She looped the grassy-scented batch over her arms, and I held open the screen door. Mom spread the curtains across the back of the davenport, ready for rehanging on freshly washed rods, against freshly washed woodwork, at freshly washed windows.

As she separated the first panel from the others, she said, "We need the blessing."

"I don't know the blessing," I said, imaging a verbal prayer—Grace Before Hanging Curtains.

"You don't know what the blessing is?" she asked, apparently surprised that a daughter of hers would not be familiar with whatever it was. She sent me to bring the straw sewing basket from the linen closet, and she put it on her lap and opened it.

I sat beside her on the divan. Inside the lid was a flowery cushion stuck with hat pins and corsage pins and threaded needles. A partitioned tray held straight pins and safety pins, wooden spools of somber-toned threads, and buttons stripped from shirts that had been torn into rags.

Mom took something shiny from the tray and handed it to me. "That is the blessing," she said.

I turned it over and over in my palm. It was thin and flat, smooth and silvery. Not longer than an inch and a half, not wider than three quarters of an inch. The bigger end looked like a rounded-off arrowhead. The other end, slightly narrower, spread open a little, like the legs of a peg clothespin.

I squeezed the parts together. "What's it for?" I asked.

Mom held the curved end of the curtain rod and pressed the open end of the blessing into the other end, and it zipped through the pocket of the curtain panel like a silver trout through a stream. "See how easy that is?" she said.

As she pushed the second curtain across the rod, she explained that, before the blessing, getting the curtains onto the rod had been a real chore. She had to go very slowly and carefully or the sharp ends of the rods would snag the curtains. The blessing was a tiny labor-saving device that made spring cleaning easier.

Mom told me to put my hand under hers at the curved end of the rod so the curtain would not slip off. Then she moved her hand to the other end, to keep the scrunched fabric from springing loose while she removed the blessing and inserted the other half of the curtain rod. As mom went to the window to snap the rod onto its brackets, I slipped the blessing into my mouth, feeling its smooth coldness, getting to know it, learning not to stick my tongue between the open prongs.

Mom evened the curtains across the width of the window and shook them so they once again billowed out like angels' gowns. Ready to thread a rod through two more panels, my mother put out her hand, tch-tched, and wiped the blessing on the hanky from her apron pocket.

"Where did it come from?" I asked her. "Why's it called a blessing?"

As she worked, Mother told me the story of how we acquired the tiny marvel.

During the Depression, before I was born, our family had been lucky. My father did not lose his job. Many gentlemen who lost their jobs tried to make a living peddling wares to housewives. The Depression men were not like the door-to-door salesmen I knew about—the ones who tried to sell my mother vacuum cleaners and Fuller brushes, the ones she told, "We don't need anything today, thank you."

The Depression peddlers went door-to-door with small kitchen utensils or handmade goods, sometimes in an old suitcase. My mother worried about their families and tried to help out by buying something from all of them. (It occurred to me that that was why we had so many potholders.)

One day, a man had come to our door carrying a satchel filled with potato peelers and sifters and funnels and other housewares. When he spread his gadgets and gizmos out on a towel, Mom noticed the shiny blunt arrow. "What is that?" she asked. The man had answered, "Madam, that is a blessing."

I suppose its proper name was something like "curtain slider" or "curtain rod smoother," but something so awesome in its simplicity and valuable in its function surely deserved an extraordinary name. Mom continued to call it the blessing. It accompanied our family to California and remained in the sewing basket for decades.

Mom kept her own house until my father died. In her early eighties, she moved into a retirement apartment where the staff cleaned her rooms. If things are not as well kept as she likes them, she doesn't complain; she is happy to have passed her chores along to someone else.

Some years ago, she gave me her old sewing basket, but the blessing was not in it. She didn't remember what had become of it. My mother is not nostalgic or sentimental. I imagine that when she no longer needed it—once curtain rods were made with smooth ends or when other draperies replaced the sheers she used to favor—she had tossed the blessing away.

I would have kept it forever, the wizard's gift that magically made my mother's work easier. Not because I needed it. Just . . . because it was a blessing to my mother.

Every few years a drapery service takes away my wilted window coverings and rehangs them, fresh and billowing. My house is not spotless as my mother's always was, and I never claimed my legacy to the Spring Cleaning Club. To me, that's a blessing.

Some things are so clearly blessings, we can call them by no other name.

• • •

AUTHOR'S NOTE:

Soon after this edition of *A Community of Voices* was published, I began my master's program in creative nonfiction, and I didn't return to the Santa Barbara Writer's Conference until many years later. I do stay in touch with Grace Rachow, the editor, but she has ceased publishing *A Community of Voices*.

From *Tiny Lights*,
"Searchlights & Signal Flares" January 2003

Contest topic: What's an Editor's Purpose?

There's no such thing as an editor.

There are editors, plural. If we imagine a singular editor, one who will do for our work what Maxwell Perkins did for Fitzgerald's and Hemingway's . . . sorry. We won't likely encounter such an editor. Rather, our work will encounter a string of editors as it makes its way from mind to keyboard to the ultimate editor in the string, the last between us and our unknown readers.

We are Editor #1. Our purpose is to review our creative work to see that it contains the indispensable admixture: basic "contest ingredients": originality, continuity, and aptness of thought; elementary craft—appropriate grammar, punctuation, and correct spelling; and applied gifts—talent and imagination.

Editor #2 might be a qualified literate friend or relative or a paid manuscript editor. No matter how well we write, we will never be the only editor we need. We believe there are things on the paper that are still in our head. We believe we have said something once that we actually said twice (because it sounded so good both ways). We believe we've proofread our work until no homophone has escaped us. We believe every pronoun is placed near its proper referent. We believe that every verb agrees with its subject and that every pronoun is in the correct case. If our piece is long enough, we will likely be wrong about every one of these beliefs. The purpose of Editor #2 is to point out the oversights of Editor #1. Our piece will go back and forth between us and Editor #2, #3, *et al.*, until we send it to the publisher of our choice.

Publishers hire multiple editors to set their expertise to our submissions. The main purpose of Editor #1P is to determine whether the material suits the needs of the publication. If she likes our piece but thinks it would require too much work, Editor #1P will use our SASE. If she likes it enough, our work will be handed to Editor #2P, and so on: the editor in charge of our genre; the acquisitions editor; the editor who designs the layout; and the final copy editor. All will apply only the skills for which they were hired.

The last of the editors is finished, and––yesss!––our name is in the table of contents. We are reading our own writing in print, yet . . . our title now contains a pun, in keeping with other titles in the publication. Our piece is shorter by 200 words, to accommodate the large white space, fonts, and illustrations that the publication features. Some of our words have been changed––also in keeping with the feel of the publication. And those "precious jewels" our early editors suggested we change, but we resisted? Gone! Words in italics or in all caps, contractions, ellipses? Those too have been changed.

      The singular editor in the query comprises many editors. If we writers are lucky enough to have our work published, most of them work for the publisher, and *their* purpose is to fulfill the objectives of the publication.

. • .

Part II, Part 2

PREVIOUSLY PUBLISHED, REVISITED

*(The unexpurgated versions,
some annotated)*

From *The Daily Pilot*

The following stories have been selected from those previously published in the *Daily Pilot,* a Community Newspaper of *the Los Angeles Times.*

Acknowledgment and gratitude are here given to John Canalis, editor of *the Daily Pilot.*

Often, the Pilot would use its own headline. In that case, I have put their headline first, separated by a colon from the title I submitted. When the two were similar, I used just my title and, of course, the publication date.

The Pilot most often edited things out of the version I submitted, according to the space available. The Pilot didn't always "get" me. Sometimes they changed things so the story no longer expressed the thought I had in mind. So what you read here will be my version. My latest version, as in I've read and changed virtually every one of these in one way or another—sometimes, just to make them fit better on the pages they consume.

In the mid-2010s, the Pilot grew from covering the Newport Beach-Costa Mesa area to covering multiple communities. They didn't increase the number of pages, so the frequency of my in-print stories decreased.

Some stories were printed online, but as the frequency of my stories being published decreased, the frequency of my submitting them also decreased.

I shall be forever grateful to John Canalis.

A Widow's Business
Widowhood Is Another Life Journey.
January 7, 2015

"It's never too late to be who you might have been."
- *George Eliot, English novelist (1819 - 1880)*

I just started taking guitar lessons. It's been 50 years since I played the guitar, and I wasn't very good then.

But, since my husband Lee died, I found I have time to do some things that I'd stopped doing, or never started doing, after we got married.

With our seven "blended" kids, I'd been busy. Across the years, our family has come to total over 30 of us, counting in-laws, grandkids, and great-grandkids. And when the patriarch died, everyone gathered 'round. It was everyone's loss.

The drama went on around me, but I felt apart from it. My mind kept returning to the seemingly countless tasks to be handled, all at once, by me—the business of being a widow.

What was involved in carrying out the directives of our trust? And what was our cash position? I had to be sure there was enough money for the current expenses, plus property taxes and income taxes. Who all needed to be notified? I knew I had to contact the Social Security Administration. But how soon?

All I'd known for sure was which mortuary would take care of Lee's body, but the number of decisions to make and forms to fill out—even just for the mortuary—stunned me.

I didn't know all that info off the top of my head!

I realized I would need to type up pages of information to keep with me, for the forms to come.

And, of course, I needed to gather what should go into Lee's obituary, plan his memorial service and the program for the guests, and . . .

Particularly during the first few weeks, I was overwhelmed by the thoughtful gifts of flowers, food, prayer cards, and contributions in Lee's name. I needed a system to keep track of that so I could write thank-you notes

When family and friends dispersed, I talked with our trust attorney and CPA, making copious notes. I needed files to keep the notes straight and easy to refer to. Things weren't imprinting on my mind as they usually did.

What was I overlooking?

Wasn't there a list of what all had to be done?

I looked for a book that would help, but nothing was like what I needed. So I made to-do lists, which grew to be 15 pages on my computer. I loosely organized the lot into TO DO - OUT and TO DO - IN.

I came to believe that what I'd learned would be helpful for others facing the matters involved in being a new widow. So I wrote the book I'd needed—*A WIDOW'S BUSINESS: A Practical Guide Through the First Year After the Death of a Spouse.*

I knew the book would be helpful for *anyone* responsible for settling someone's estate, but I liked my title. Whether you're a widow, a widower, an executor, a relative—I think of those things that have to be done as *business*, a widow's business.

I organized the material into sections, according to priority as I'd learned the priorities. Before I'd finished, friends began requesting the information for their friends and relatives.

One fellow suggested I write an article about my experiences, and that's why this peculiar piece is in your newspaper.

Maybe you are a widow and way past this, but many widows' (and non-widows') friends become widows—or widowers, or executors—and can use some help.

Everyone should know that help is at hand, whether it comes in a comprehensive book, or from calling your trust attorney or CPA, or by asking a widow you know.

Help is at hand. You can do this!

And when the dust settled, a year or so after Lee's death, I realized that I have life ahead of me and a future to plan for!

The time had come for me to rediscover what it was I "might have been." Maybe someone who plays the guitar and sings along, just for herself. Maybe somebody who writes another book.

There are lots of things to do and to be, even later in life.

• • •

Kind Words Exchanged—50 Years After Our Divorce
January 27, 2015

I went to see my ex-husband (E-H) in the hospital Sunday. I've had as little interaction with him as possible since our divorce in 1965, considering that we share two children.

But last Sunday, I was having breakfast with my son Mark, who was visiting from his neck of the Greater L.A.-Orange County woods, and he mentioned that his father was in Hoag Hospital.

That's my bailiwick! E-H lives in Huntington Beach, on the other side of Hoag.

"Hey," I said. "Shall we go see him?"

Mark had been closer to Lee, his stepfather, than to his own father, but Mark has been dutiful in E-H's later years.

"Sure," he said.

I had last seen E-H several years ago, at my sons' stepmother's home. Son Tim and I had gone there to pick up Mark for a trip to a family Christmas gathering.

"Who's that old man?" I'd asked Edna.

"The boys' father," she said.

Wow. E-H had looked older than Lee, who was 15 years older than both of us. Maybe having an older husband made me forget what men my age look like, but I don't think so.

Clearly, E-H had some health issues, and they ultimately landed him in Hoag this week. I greeted him with, "What are you doing in my neighborhood?"

He actually had a funny retort. Wish I could remember it, but I was more focused on thinking he looked better than he had a few years earlier. Lost weight. Not so pasty.

He said, "How are you getting along since Lee . . . ?"

He meant *died* but didn't say it.

"I am doing OK," I said. "I've accepted it. Lee wasn't going to get better when *he* was here, like you will."

A nurse came in then and said E-H would be moved shortly to a rehabilitation hospital. He'd have physical therapy there and then go home in a few days. She'd directed her comments to me, as if I were responsible for him. "Tell his son," I said.

I wrote the address down on the inside cover of a crossword puzzles book. The pen I'd picked up had nearly run out of ink.

The phone rang, and E-H conversed with his daughter, Mark's half-sister. He told her he would be at Hoag for several more days, *not* that he was about to be transferred to rehab.

Mark called Kathleen back, explained things, and gave her the address, which I'd written over with a pen I carried in my purse. I told E-H I'd leave him the pen for his puzzles.

When the nurse was gone, it occurred to me that I might not have another chance to see E-H again. Yes, he would recover. But the odds of my seeing him again were slim, and it suddenly popped into my head that I had something to tell him.

"Before I go," I said, "I want to thank you for Tim and Mark."

He paused for a while for that to sink in. Then he said the kindest words he'd ever spoken to me: "I thank *you*."

Some spontaneous actions seem almost inspired, and I will always be glad that I went to see him and that we were able to thank each other for the goodness that came from our brief, unhappy marriage.

• • •

Having Fun at the LA Times Festival of Books
Thanks for the umbrella, but when will it rain?
Easter Sunday, April 24th, 2015

Last Sunday, my son and I went to The Los Angeles Times Festival of Books. We'd enjoyed much of the day at the stage presentations and were trying to catch an author before the event ended to sign some books Mark had bought earlier.

As he forged ahead, I was distracted by a fantastic umbrella at the LA Times booth. The umbrella, patterned with comic strips from the Times, was hanging above the heads of the last few folks milling around inside the booth.

"What a wonderful umbrella!" I said aloud, imagining carrying it on a coming trip to the British Isles.

A woman in a Times t-shirt approached me.

"I love that umbrella," I said. "Is it for sale?"

"No," she said. "It's for new subscribers. Would you like to sign up to take The Times?"

"Oh, my dear, I have been a subscriber to the Times since . . . 1960," I said, thinking back to when I was a newly married woman (the first time).

"Since 1960!" she said. "Over 50 years!"

"Yes," I said. "And I pay full fare. I want the Times to be delivered in print forever!"

She looked at me for a long moment and went to get an unopened umbrella from the few remaining. "You deserve this," she said. "But don't tell anyone I gave it to you."

It was the end of the last day, after all. How many new subscribers were they expecting to get in the next half hour? Still, I thanked her profusely. And I hid the umbrella diagonally inside my sweater—or most of it. The handle stuck out five inches to the northwest of the top, and the pointy end stuck out another five inches southeast.

A half hour or so later, Mark and I were ready to leave and had to walk past the Times booth again. This time, a young man there confronted me. "Where did you get that umbrella?"

"What umbrella" I answered, straight-faced.

"The umbrella you're hiding," he said.

"I don't have an umbrella," I said.

"Yes you do!" he insisted, not understanding that I was kidding him.

"Maybe I stole it," I said.

"Did you?" he asked, also straight-faced.

"No."

"Then where did you get it," he persisted.

"I promised I wouldn't tell anyone," I said. "I begged for it because I love it so much and because I have been a subscriber to the Times for over 50 years."

The fellow looked at me out of the corner of his eyes, as if he wasn't sure I *hadn't* stolen the umbrella. I can't imagine what he was planning to do if I had.

I said, "Now you have made me lose my son! I will not have a ride home!"

"Your son will wait for you," he said, maybe not sure about that or maybe not sure I had a son at all.

"I have to hurry along," I said.

"Well," he called after me, "you'd better keep subscribing!"

When I showed my friend Jeanne my delightful umbrella, I acknowledged that I couldn't possibly carry it to Europe. It's 33 inches long. It would never fit into my suitcase, let alone be small enough to carry sightseeing.

"It is a big one!" she said. "Maybe it is a golfing umbrella. The long tip is for sticking it into the grass."

Not being a golfer, I wouldn't know. And though I'll never take my wonderful umbrella traveling, I do love it and am eager to use it. There's plenty of room for two under it.

But the Southern California drought seems endless! When is it going to rain?!

• • •

AFTER STORY:
Unbeknownst to me, John Canalis, the editor of the Daily Pilot, sent my story to the Vendor Sales Department of the Times in downtown LA.

Two days after I'd submitted the article, I received a package from the LA Times, with a lovely note from Kelli Rizzi. She said, "I met a lot of people at the Festival of Books, and yet I remember you. Safe travels!"

And in the package was a *travel-size* comic-strip-patterned umbrella!!

What Really IS in a Name?
What's in a name? More than you might think.
Sunday, May 24, 2015

Why isn't my name Paige? Or Regina? Or another pretty name? An uncommon name. A sophisticated name.

My mother named me Mary Elizabeth. I have never liked my name. In 1939, Mary was the most popular name for baby girls. Where I grew up, it seemed every girl's first name was Mary Something. Mary was almost not a real name—more like Mrs. or Miss. Or Sister.

In high school, a boyfriend nicknamed me Mary Liz, but I never liked that either. It sounded back-woodsy.

As an adult, I had only sons. I never got to name a girl baby, but I surely wouldn't have named her after myself!

After my divorce, when I applied for a job, the guy who hired me said, "You're hired. What do people call you?"

"Mary Elizabeth," I shrugged.

After a pause, he said, "We will call you Liz."

I liked it. It went well with my then last name. It goes well with my current last name. But it's harsh. It isn't "me." I often sign notes Lizzie. I like the idea of being an old lady named Lizzie, so I'm breaking it in now.

As my mother aged, her short term memory got shorter. I had always felt bad because I hadn't fulfilled one of her life's wishes: that all of her children would graduate from college. So I graduated from college at the age of 59. When she saw my diploma, in the name of Mary E. Newman, Mother said, "That isn't your name."

When my writing partner Bill Thomas and I self-published a college English text book, I thought my mother would be thrilled. I said, "Look, Mother. I've published a book!" When she saw the co-author's name of Liz Newman, she said, "That isn't your name." My writing partner and I sold our self-published book to Harcourt-Brace, and I listed my name as Liz Swiertz Newman. When Mother saw that cover, she smiled and nodded and said, "Good for you, sweetie."

OK, then. Liz Swiertz Newman it shall be.

My mother lived to be a hundred. In her last years, she was quite hard of hearing and beyond being able to take the tests for hearing aids. My sister Carolyn and I communicated with her by means of a white board. It was easier to get her talking and to respond to her rather than for her to respond to questions, which she either couldn't hear or couldn't absorb. One day, I wrote on the white board, "Ray and Carolyn."

Mother said, "Oh, those are my children! How do you know them?"

That was somewhat disconcerting, but, I could imagine that she remembered me as a child, not my 60-plus self. I wrote on the white board "Mary Elizabeth."

My mother cocked her head, a puzzled look on her face. "I don't know her," she said, "but that is a *very* pretty name."

So, that is why my name isn't Paige.

• • •

There are trips, and then there are vacations.
June 6, 2015

The thing about travel is that you must know at the planning stage whether you want to go on a trip or a vacation. A trip involves sightseeing and cramming as much as possible into the time allotted, including souvenir shopping. A vacation involves lying in the shade on a chaise, reading a novel or doing a crossword puzzle, and sipping umbrella drinks.

If you and your traveling companion aren't in accord, it leads to the expectations of one or the other not being met (with accompanying ill feelings).

Once my husband and I figured this out, we alternated trips with vacations. Previously, I would be champing at the bit and rarin' to go, while Lee would be lolling about as though time were not of the essence.

I just got back from my first trip since Lee died. Son Mark and I took a cruise around the British Isles. Prior to leaving, I experienced some tension and anxiety. However, Mark is fun to be with, and we laughed ourselves silly, starting on the airplane.

Maybe this is something you had to be there to appreciate, but I'll test it on you.

We were settled into business class, having just been served our drinks—a Manhattan for me and Scotch and water for Mark. Usually the first thing I do is thumb through the airline's magazine and the Duty Free catalog, but with no seat pocket in front of me, it appeared there were neither.

I said, "Oh, they don't have any airplane magazines," and Mark said, "Yes, they do. They're between us, behind us." And he gestured across his chest with his Scotch and water, sloshing it all over his jacket.

I said (of course), "Oh, Mark! you've spilled your drink!"

And Mark quickly said, "It's OK, Mom. The jacket is waterproof . . . and now it has been SCOTCH guarded!"

I laughed so hard I was squeaking out sounds and gasping for breath. Laughter is a great release from the tension of catching an airplane.

So, did you need to be there to find that funny?

Deep laughter is a great release.

Everything would be OK.

We didn't have time to explore London—not even the outside of the Tower of London. We did walk from the hotel to the Thames so we could see Big Ben and the giant Ferris wheel called the London Eye. It was a long walk, over an hour. Clearly, my long-distance fast-walking days are over.

As I was jet-lagged and spent, we flagged down a taxi on the bridge across the Thames, which is probably illegal. A lovely young driver rescued us.

I told him where we wanted to go and that I had a problem: I had no pounds with which to pay him. I had 20 Euros, a credit card, and American money. He said the ride would probably cost about 15 pounds, and he didn't take Euros or credit cards, but he would stop where I could use a currency exchange machine.

I said, "I am exhausted, and I will give you 40 American dollars if you will pay for the ride yourself."

He recognized the very good deal (the pound was worth about 1.65 dollars), and I surely got my money's worth. Mark and I agreed it was what Dad would have done.

After our auspicious start, everything continued to go smoothly. I carried my wonderful LA Times comics-patterned umbrella on each excursion, but it virtually never rained except when we were on a coach. I finally asked Mark to take a photo of me inside the coach with my umbrella open. I'll have to send a copy to my new friend in the LA Times Vendor Sales.

All along, Mark and I were of a mind as to the purpose of our adventure. We crammed in every possible sight we could in the two-week period, including a six-hour round-trip bus ride to spend five hours in Paris, with a cruise along the Seine.

We visited many places we had never been. Guernsey. Blarney Castle in Cork—Mark made the grueling climb up its tower, but I did not. (Although I didn't witness it, I tell people that when Mark kissed the Blarney Stone, it kissed him back.) Dublin. Belfast. Glasgow. The Orkney Islands. Inverness—the Loch Ness monster remained submerged. Edinburgh.

Highlights: Foreign accents, green scenery, castles and cathedrals, the beer and Scotch distilleries, the Royal Yacht Britannia in the Port of Leith (Lee's real name), and local souvenirs.

We returned home worn out—but both of us thoroughly satisfied.

A trip to remember.

But definitely not a vacation!

• • •

The Case of the Missing Plug Nickels
July 10, 2015

My friend Jeanne and I used to play Nancy Drew when we were kids. We were lucky to grow up three doors apart from each other in Los Angeles and are luckier still to be neighbors now.

When we were young, there was so much to do! No supervised play dates or organized girls' sports. No gymnastics or karate lessons. Just the freedom to be kids. (Son Tim says his was the last generation to experience that kind of freedom.)

The world was safer then.

Summer was free time for running through the sprinklers, playing with dolls under the fruit trees in our backyards, and playing hide-and-seek until dark. Weekends were for free shows at the Ritz, the La Brea, and the El Rey.

We lived on Citrus Avenue, near Wilshire and Highland, a few blocks from the Miracle Mile, a block and a half from the creek. I suppose the creek had a name, but we just called it the creek. It was down low in someone's back yard, off of 8th Street, and nobody stopped us from wading in the cool water and catching crawfish in Hills Bros. coffee cans. It's fenced off now.

Of course, whether on weekends or in the summer, we could also roller skate, ride our bikes, and explore.

Before we had bikes, we kept our eyes on the sidewalk so we wouldn't step on any cracks. Sometimes we would find a penny or a nickel or a dime along the way. With all that exercise, it's no wonder we were skinny then.

We Citrus Avenue girls—Jeanne, Sharon, Mary Ellyn, and I—could wander anywhere within our purview: west on Wilshire Boulevard, past Kress and Woolworth's, to the Tar Pits; north of there to the Farmers Market at 3rd and Fairfax to watch the cake decorators or share a piece of black bottom pie; southeast to the Public Library across from LA High on Olympic (where we took swimming lessons); west to the crafts program at Wilshire Crest playground, where Jeanne always beat me at tether ball; then to Currie's—with a dime tied in the corner of our hankies—for a mile-high fudge-ripple ice cream cone or a "Green River" or a cherry phosphate.

It was the era of Punch & Judy's ice cream parlor, where once in a while Sharon's dad would take us for an Idiot's Delight.

The most fun was exploring houses being built. After World War II there were a lot of them. We would pretend we were looking for clues to solve a mystery—maybe "The Secret of the Framed House." Jeanne and I felt we were doing something very dangerous, although we were always cautious.

We would collect the plugs punched out of newly installed electrical boxes. Jeanne and I kept ours in empty Band-Aid boxes. Shaking them made such a delightful racket! The boys said they used the plugs, or slugs, in jawbreaker machines. We didn't tell on them, though.

More than 50 miles south (and considerably more than 50 years later), Jeanne and I are still lured to houses under construction. And we still refer to it as "playing Nancy Drew" when we make a date to explore after the workmen have gone home.

A major remodel has been going on next door since last November. Jeanne and I played Nancy Drew and explored it not long ago. It was fun observing the clues and guessing where the kitchen would be now, figuring out the newly designed location of the hall bath and the master suite, and enjoying the view, which would be visible from a whole corner of windows.

We didn't find any plugs, though. Where could they have gone? Don't they make electrical boxes like that anymore?

Being a grown-up takes some of the adventure out of things. Before we went, I'd asked Suzy, the owner, if it would be all right if I walked through her project as it progressed.

She said, "Yes, just be careful."

And of course Nancy J and Nancy L have always been careful, since the beginning of their partnership.

• • •

Red Light, Green Light—On Demand
Impatient for Red Lights
to Turn Green in My Direction
July 17, 2015

When I was in my teens, Bill Stulla hosted a kids' TV show called "Cartoon Express." I was too old for the show, but somehow I and my friends learned of his milk-drinking game, called Red Light, Green Light.

We played it in Balboa when my parents chaperoned some of us there for a week. At sixteen, my friends and I were still drinking milk when we ate our Wheaties.

When it was my turn to be "Engineer Bill," it was fun to make the red lights short and the green lights long.

I used to work for a firm of traffic engineers. When Lee and I first moved to Corona del Mar in 2002, we were thrilled at the way traffic moved. "Sneaky Pete" right turn lanes and 50- and 55-miles-per-hour speed limits. And what my former traffic engineer employer referred to as "responsive" traffic signals, which turn green for waiting drivers when there is no interfering traffic.

What a concept!

The light at Crown Drive and San Joaquin Hills seemed to respond to the snap of my fingers.

I used to joke that Gelson's paid for a responsive signal at the corner of San Miguel and San Joaquin Hills, for the convenience of its customers.

Then, the road work. Lots of long-lasting road work. After which, no more green-light convenience for shoppers stopping at Gelson's on their way home.

Turning left in any direction at San Miguel and SJH, you could contemplate the sunset and what's for dinner and who might be playing the Angels tonight—while no cars are visible in any direction and you have to wait for an eventual spurt of oncoming traffic to pass through the intersection before you get the green arrow.

These days, a left turn at MacArthur and SJH, and then at San Miguel and SJH, can take five minutes. Really? Yes.

Think of all that wasted gas!

To avoid the longest-wait signals, I learned to take Bonita Canyon/Ford Road/San Miguel coming home, and if it wasn't time for moms to pick up their kids at school, I'd turn onto Pacific View from San Miguel, where you didn't even have to wait for a green arrow.

Then, alas, at Marguerite and San Joaquin Hills, the last responsive signal capitulated to some arbitrary timing design.

I assume it's not just Corona del Mar's drivers but all of Newport Beach's that have the irritating problem of waiting and waiting for lights to change.

And while we're at it, why shouldn't facing left-turn lanes both move at the same time?

OK, I sound like I am having a tantrum—even though I am grown up, or at least an adult. I don't drink milk anymore. But when it's my turn at the traffic signals, I want the red lights to be short and the green lights to be long—in my direction. Or, preferably, just responsive to the traffic or lack of it.

Come on, City of Newport Beach traffic engineers! Please give some attention to this stressful, gas-wasting, time-wasting situation!

• • •

Singing the Praises of the Orange County Fair
A Trip to the Orange County Fair
Brings Back Plenty of Memories.
August 4, 2015

I've always loved going to a fair. The first movies I remember was "State Fair"(1945) with Jeanne Crain, Dick Haymes, and Percy Kilbride. The mother submits mincemeat for judging (that gets spiked with booze) and the father submits his prize pig (who falls in love with a competitor pig and mopes). The son gets back at the midway pitchman who cheated him the previous year, and the daughter falls in love. Ahhh.

The movie featured great Rogers and Hammerstein songs, like "It Might as Well Be Spring" and "It's a Grand Night for Singing." Watch it next time it shows up on TCM!

Lee and I used to take our family to the LA County Fair—the Disneyland of county fairs. But with our kids off to college and then moving hither and thither and beginning their own families, the tradition faded. After we moved to Newport Beach, Lee became unable to amble through that giant of all fairs, and we hadn't been there in years. We tried the OC Fair a couple times, but even it became too much for my darling husband.

Saturday, son Mark and I went to the OC Fair, which is like a little brother to its kin to the north.

OMGoodness! What a plethora of things to do and see! We started with the photography displays, particularly enjoying the photos taken by youngsters (under 18). It's always a treat to see old things through young eyes, and the kids who presented their photos for judging took marvelous shots.

I was surprised at the quantity of photography displayed —bigger, I think, than the display at the bigger brother's fair.

We also looked at the carved wood displays, the quilting and other needlework displays, and the floral arrangements and table settings. What talent the people have who submitted their gorgeous work to be judged and for all of us to see!

I would have given anyone who submitted anything at least an Honorable Mention ribbon.

Mark and I especially enjoyed the "it slices, it dices" demonstrations in the product buildings. It has been a family tradition to buy something at every fair that we will never use. Three items have a chance at that honor this year.

First I bought a fantastic mop that comes with an infinity-shaped bucket, with water for the mop at one side and a wringer like a salad spinner at the other. The easy-on/easy-off mop head is made with micro fibers that spin damp dry! So cool.

I also bought some magic stretchy-substance covers for saving leftovers in the refrigerator and to use for nuking, plus a bundle of really neat slide-on package-closers—way better than chip clips.

What a kick! And what a good sport Mark was to carry it all around. Including the mop and bucket.

We also bought some for-sure useful stuff—like an ionic anklet that would help me keep my balance as I get older. And I bought a pair of sandals. At the 5-hours-of-walking point, I had to buy sandals or house slippers or I couldn't have gone on.

Seems to me we stopped to eat or drink something between every major attraction.

We ate delightfully disgusting things. I tried deep-fried curly zucchini, but I had to quit after consuming about a quarter cup of fry oil. Mark had a three-tiered cheeseburger with glazed donuts for the bun. All part of the fun.

Fortunately, we chased that fat through our system periodically—first at the wine tasting (chili cheese dogs are a good pairing), later by sharing a "Rum Runner," and last with an ordinary beer. I didn't even have room for a funnel cake!

Finding an empty table in the shade was next to impossible, but other fair visitors were welcoming when we asked to join them. We chatted with people from distant parts of Orange County, and I was particularly enchanted with twin girls, about five, one of whom asked, "How about you be my neighbor?" Of course I told her I would *love* to be her neighbor.

We never got to the pig races, but I don't think we missed a crafter or a shop, and it was well after 6:00 when we got back to my house. We'd walked a ton, gotten lots of fresh air and sunshine, and laughed a lot.

Mark and I agreed that next time we should go later in the day and stay until dark, when the lights go on and the colorful, shining attractions of the midway come alive.

It's a grand night for singing . . .

• • •

AFTER STORY:

My housekeepers declared that the mop never gets dry enough to use on the wood floors. (I suspect the *demo* mop's fibers and the *purchased* mop's fibers might have been different fibers.)

The stretchy tops for containers are never the size I need.

The slip-on "chip clips" are really great!

I haven't tumbled over anything, and it could be the anklet. Or maybe the anklet reminds me to be more careful.

And the comfortable sandals quickly became my favorite pair. The Sandalman's shop is located on Superior in Newport Beach. Look him up!

An Embarrassment of Photographic Riches
August 20, 2015

I recently got the last of the British Isles prints from snapfish.com. My camera had given out on Day 3 of our recent trip around the British Isles, so I had to rely on my son Mark's electronic devices.

Wow, have things changed since Lee and I used to travel. Bless his heart, he would carry a ton of equipment for me—my single lens reflex with the normal lens, plus the wide-angle lens and the foot-long lens that weighed a lot but took stunning close-ups of distant things. I had to select my own f-stops back then.

And film?! Oh, my gosh! When I was packing for a trip, I would take the film out of the bright yellow boxes and number a sticker on each canister, which Lee toted around the world for me in that same hefty camera case. As I exposed each roll, I wrote what was on it beneath the number, then loaded the next numbered roll.

And developing was costly back then! A traveler tended to be specific in her choice of shots.

I have bought successively smaller, simpler cameras over the years. On one of our last cruises, I bought a shiny red slim-line camera, but Lee and I just went to Hawaii after that, and you only need so many pics of palm trees and gorgeous beaches and stunning turquoise water.

To document our trips, we relied on the ship's photographers' pictures of our disembarking in the different ports, plus the formal photos. We bought the ones I thought "turned out well." I am the least photogenic person I know. In the port pics, I am usually wearing sunglasses, which helps.

The shiny red camera had a design defect, IMHO. It turned on when the cover was slid open, and this seemed to occur randomly in my purse, without my consent. As a result, the battery was frequently drained when I needed it.

I made it a point not to let that happen on the British Isles trip, and I charged the battery dutifully each night, but the camera apparently resented having its freedom curtailed and its battery simply quit holding a charge. The photography studio on the ship didn't sell batteries. By Day 3, the only cameras left for sale were in the over-$400 range. I was in the under-that range.

So Mark took the pictures. His electronics consisted of a nice little camera with an on/off switch and a zoom lens—very serviceable. He also took photos on his iPad. And on his phone.

I rather enjoyed not taking the pictures. I didn't have to see everything through the eye of the camera for a change.

The first batch of pictures that he transferred to my home computer, over a month ago, were from his camera. I had already loaded the 100 or so I had taken, compared similar shots, and deleted the less-good ones. As I recall, the total number of pictures I loaded onto snapfish, just from our cameras, was in excess of 750.

I winnowed that number down to approximately 600, editing as I went through them, and ordered two of each. I bet you have no idea how much 1200 photos weigh. I had to get the dolly from the garage.

When the crate was opened, I couldn't begin to guess what order the twenty or so fat packets went in. When did we go there? I remember that! Where was it?

I don't wish to sound jaded, but the insides of one castle or cathedral can look much like the insides of another, once things get out of order. As for scenery, in the British Isles, it is green everywhere, and whether the animals are cows or sheep doesn't help identify where the tour bus was headed. The beautiful buildings looked similar in all the ports, too . . .

Mark and I spent a Sunday putting the pics in the same order as on his laptop. What a relief. I wrote where and when on all the envelopes, times two.

Then he put the iPad pictures on my computer. We agreed to not load the phone pictures. There weren't many of those anyway.

After I uploaded the iPad pictures to snapfish, it took me days to go through them—and not consecutive days—selecting the better of similar shots. When my eyes began spinning in my head, I gave up and ordered all of the rest of them. Two each. They're here. Waiting for a Sunday visit from my traveling companion, when all we have to do is sort through pictures.

Then to get all the photos culled and put into albums!

Meanwhile, I bought a new camera, with an extra battery. I'm sure I'll go somewhere within the year. And no more dolly-loads of snapshot deliveries from now on. I'll stick to taking pictures with family or friends in them. The sights will be recorded for all time, but in the background.

• • •

Growing Up, Then and Now, Ready or Not
July 30, 2015

People talk about where they "grew up." I spent my memorable childhood years, from 7 to 12, living at 725 South Citrus Avenue, Los Angeles, in the 1950s. That's where I supposedly grew up.

But I've had three major growth spurts since then.

The first time I was married, it was for all the wrong reasons—because everyone else was doing it, because it would be nice to have a pretty wedding, to entertain friends in my own home. To be able to say to my husband, "Honey, would you get some more ice for the drinks?"

He also got married for the wrong reasons. He wanted to have two kids in order to avoid the draft. When you think about it, he was the more successful of the two of us.

When he left, I was 25, and I had never been on my own. I had two small sons, not much child support, and too much stubbornness to ask my parents for help. My mother hadn't wanted me to marry so young, especially not to someone utterly without financial promise. No college degree. No expectation of meaningful employment.

Still, we'd managed. In the early sixties, it hadn't cost so much to live. Even my under-educated and under-job-gifted husband could support us and our two sons. And, with help from his family, we had just moved into our own minuscule home in the Valley.

A couple months later, "See ya around, babe."

Now in charge: under-educated, under-job-gifted *me*.

I hadn't worked in five years! My typing skills were rusty. And nobody used a Dictaphone anymore.

How would I manage?!

I found a crummy minimum-wage job, but in the time I worked there, I matured more than in the previous ten years.

My self-esteem recovered. I was worth *more* than having a husband who didn't care about me, worth *more* than being someone's better—but useless and unfulfilled—half.

It was gratifying to receive a paycheck, to pay the mortgage, buy the food, pay for childcare, and even buy my first car, which provided fantastic, new-to-me freedom.

My bosses appreciated me. They taught me book-keeping and how to wire a business switchboard. Within two years, they'd doubled my minimum-wage starting salary.

Maybe that job wasn't so crummy after all!

Discovering that I was of value and I could take care of myself and my sons, without anyone's help, was a true growth experience.

When I got married the second time, it was for the right reasons. Lee was everything my former husband was not. He was mature, stable, fun, a homebody, and we loved each other! He was a wonderful husband and friend.

He taught me so much about being a parent and about how to be a wife to a nice guy!

From parenting each other's kids to traveling everywhere after he retired . . . I loved our partnership. We were married for 45 years. While I grew in those years, the changes were gradual.

My third growth spurt began nearly two years ago, when Lee died.

I had leaned on him for 60 percent of my life. Before that, I'd never lived alone. I'd barely spent a night alone! Yes, I did take care of the household and the bank accounts, but all that became daunting once I didn't have Lee to consult. Should I buy the new air conditioning unit with a 5-year guarantee, or should I pay for the repairs that have a 2-year guarantee? Etc.

To say nothing of the countless other tasks and decisions I faced that first year.

During our marriage, I'd finally received my BA. I even got my MFA. Yet not all that schooling, nor 45 years of time passing, contributed as much to my growing up as two years without Lee.

I am self-reliant. I can manage money. I can make decisions. (I bought the new air conditioner.) I know whom to go to for advice when it's needed.

I might be approaching little-old-lady-hood, but I can handle nearly anything by myself.

I wish I'd never had to experience life without Lee. But two years later, I feel that growing up some more is a very positive thing.

So if you ask where I grew up, I could say "Los Angeles . . . and the San Fernando Valley . . . and Corona del Mar."

And wherever comes next on my growth chart.

• • •

Last one out of the 20th century, turn off the lights!
Technology May Be Advancing,
but I'd Rather Stay Put.
August 27, 2015

I've heard that to *have* a ship inside a bottle, the ship has to have been *built* inside the bottle. Seems awfully hard. Why bother?

Throughout our married life, in addition to the seven children we raised together, Lee and I tended to "adopt" especially bright and lovable young people. One of them is our computer guru, Brian.

He has been an invaluable support since 2004, retrieving information and repairing, updating, and replacing our computers and modems. Now he even does "odd" jobs for me, like finding a speaker for my new television. (I cannot understand why I need a separate speaker to understand the sound on my new television.)

So today, when Brian finished with the speaker, he raised a subject I have been resisting all the years I have known him.

Let it be known that throughout my older-middle years (age 45-60), I was into learning new things.

I was the one who set the clocks on the digital devices. I was the one who learned how to tape record television shows. I was the one who explained over and over to Lee how to turn the TV on and off with the Cox remote.

I was quickly into word processing on a computer, years before the Internet and email. I had a cell phone hard wired into my car before any of my friends.

But, in my younger-older years (age 60-75?), I said, Stop. No more new technology. I'm too busy to learn it.

My friend Marian did convince me to get a portable cell phone about 20 years ago, but I only used it to call Lee to tell him I was headed home.

For those 20 years, I had an AT&T plan that cost me $20 a month, and I only charged the phone if I thought I might use it. When Lee died, Jan and Cheryl insisted I get an iPhone. I protested that instead of a $20 plan and an uncharged phone, I would have a $70 plan and an uncharged phone.

I gave in to my daughters' cajoling, and that's what happened. I've resisted learning to use it.

So Brian raised the subject I was even *less* willing to consider, "transitioning to a new server." What he meant was it was time for me to abandon AOL, the only server I'd ever used, to abandon the only email address I'd ever had. I put my hands over my ears.

It seemed like a change of subject when he asked me if I had a website. I actually have three websites—one for my name and two for books. My son Tim told me I needed a website for the book I published in 2013, and he taught me how to accomplish that on GoDaddy.com. He spent four hours on the phone with me while I did it.

"Three websites," Brian said. "You know, you could consolidate those sites with a parent-type site and have contacts from them forwarded to one server, something more professional-sounding than AOL.com. AOL is a dinosaur. The rest of the world is moving on without you, Liz."

"Did I ever tell you why I quit guitar lessons?" I asked him.

"I didn't know you'd quit guitar," he said.

"I quit because the teacher wanted me to move faster than I wanted to. I wanted to strum 'Ghostriders in the Sky," and he wanted me to do all this fancy flamenco fingering. Ruined it for me. That's where you are headed, Brian."

"No, Liz! You can do this. It's easier than you think!"

I watched Brian and *his* magic fingering as he keyed his way to GoDaddy and tended to business.

I kept shaking my head. "What you're trying to do, Brian—instead of building the ship inside the bottle—is push the ship into the bottle, and it doesn't want to go!"

Brian laughed at the metaphor. "I've been pushing it for over ten years, Liz. I think it's just about ready to join the flotilla with the rest of us."

I thought that was a very clever continuation of the analogy, and I let it suck me at least part way in.

Four hours later, I had a new website. I had a new email address. I had a basic understanding of how the new server works, and I admitted to Brian that it's relatively easy, way more functional, and a really good idea.

When all of me is inside that bottle, I suppose I will start using my cell phone.

Before Brian left, he checked the shower head, which he'd overheard my housekeeper Amanda tell me was leaking. He said the problem is in the valve.

Tomorrow I call the plumber. He never tries to teach me anything.

• • •

My Place
Recording Life's Milestones in a Special Restaurant
August 31, 2015

Lots of people have a place where they are the most comfortable, where they feel at home, and I do not mean on the couch in front of their TV. Some other place. Their place. A peaceful, happy place where they feel like they belong. Maybe it's a shady bench in the park or on the sand by the ocean at sunset.

My place is a restaurant not far from where I live. Lee and I enjoyed it because it is noted for two of my favorites, steak and martinis, and because the library dining room is just a few steps from the valet. On the same level is a patio, and though I love to dine *al fresco* and the patio is lovely, we preferred "our" booth.

It's quiet in the library—maybe the only quiet dining place in town. Other diners prefer upstairs where it is lively, or they don't know about downstairs, but Lee and I preferred the library, which was often empty except for us. We called it our private dining room.

We went there frequently for about ten years, sometimes twice a week. We came to know the manager, the owners, the servers—the same employees all those years.

The busboys, brothers Roberto and Augusto, always bring my water without ice, the way I like it. When Mark was divorced, they helped him move his things with their truck.

I cannot count the number of family events we've celebrated there. When I call and identify myself, whoever answers the phone says, "Oh, Mrs. Newman! We'll look forward to seeing you again."

On the Friday Lee died, I made dinner reservations there for our family members who had gathered. I explained to David, the manager, why we would be coming.

When we arrived, an arrangement of blue hydrangeas and other fresh flowers was in the center of our table. Paul, Marty, Bobby, Sean, and Linda all came to give me a hug. I introduced them to our children. David told us that Jim and Lou were comping my dinner and a round of drinks for the six of us who'd gathered.

David handed me a beautiful sympathy card that everyone who worked at the restaurant had signed. Even Mike-the-valet and the chefs. And they didn't just sign their names. Each of them wrote something personal and kind about Lee or about the two of us as a couple.

Linda wrote, "This is a safe place for you. We care about you here."

So this restaurant is *my place*. I continue to go there often. I love to introduce friends to the restaurant and to the people who make it my place.

When I'm with a couple of my kids or friends, we still sit inside, in "my" booth, where Lee and I always sat.

Friday night, one of my daughters and I went there to celebrate the publication of my book.

The guys dropped by to say hi as they passed on their way to serve the guests on the patio. Jim stopped to ask what we had been toasting. "To success," I said. "I just published my book!" When the check came, Paul said Jim had comped our desserts because we'd come there to celebrate.

Every time I go there it's a celebration. It's like it says in that song from "Cheers," the old TV show. Sometimes you just need to be where you're recognized and welcomed. That's the kind of place my place is.

Oh, and they have excellent steaks, the best lobster in town, and darn good martinis.

• • •

AFTER STORY:
The name of the restaurant is The Bungalow, near the corner of Pacific Coast Highway and Carnation Avenue in Corona del Mar. I was afraid that if I used the name of the restaurant in the story, the Daily Pilot might not publish it.

The fun thing is that, after the piece was published, lots of people came up to me, either guessing what the restaurant is or asking what it is. So my place got its publicity anyway.

I still dine there with family and friends, still celebrate anything worth celebrating there, and even when I go alone, I'm always among friends.

It *is* a safe place for me.

Family Discussion on Water Conservation
An Old Trick Will Help You Conserve Water.
September 13, 2015

My daughters and I went out to brunch on Sunday. When Jan and Cheryl and I are together, our conversation topics hop all over the place. After we got back to my house, I mentioned that I had a leak in the shower, and I was carrying the bucket from the shower to the toilet to the shower and back again.

Cheryl laughed, and Jan said, "What are you talking about?"

"The bucket. I bought two and gave one to Cheryl."

"But what do you mean—shower, toilet, shower?" Jan persisted.

"She lets the water from the leak drip into the bucket, then uses the water to flush the toilet."

"And I collect the water when I shower."

Jan still didn't understand. "What does it have to do with pouring it down the toilet?"

"We're in the fifth year of a drought and we have water restrictions here. To conserve, the bucket in the shower collects extra water, and I use it to flush the toilet," I explained.

"But there is already water in the toilet. I don't understand."

"You use the water in the bucket *instead of* the water in the toilet tank to flush the toilet. You know, after you've used the toilet." Cheryl explained.

"I don't get it."

I explained further. "Dad taught me this a long time ago. If your toilet is clogged, you can clear it by pouring a whole bucket of water into the bowl."

Cheryl said, "The force of a lot of water pushes everything through."

Jan said, "I am not getting this. Can you just show me?"

"Follow me," I said.

The three of us strode into the back bathroom.

"Bucket of water," I said, retrieving the bucket from the shower. "The plumber can't come until Tuesday."

"Bucket. I've got that," Jan said.

"Toilet," I said. I lifted the seat. "Observe."

I put a square of toilet paper into the toilet and poured in about a quart of water.

Swoooosh, went the toilet.

"Oh, for heaven's sake," Jan said.

Cheryl said, "In your house, what with the live-in kids and the grandkids you babysit, you can save a lot of tank water."

We returned to the den and put our feet back up on the coffee table.

"The kids' bathroom has a door to the outside," Jan said. "They could water the plants with shower water."

"If it's not too soapy," Cheryl said.

"Or," I said, "they can flush their toilet."

"But I have low flow toilets," Jan said.

"But they still use extra water to flush," I said.

Cheryl got up to leave. "Ugh. I cannot believe we are still discussing this subject. You should just write a story about it," she said.

"Excellent idea," I said. "And it might inspire other people to re-use their shower water."

• • •

The thrill is gone, except vicariously.
Shopping—and Bonding—Through the Ages
September 15, 2016

How I used to love to shop! As a young girl, it was a thrill to get a new dress for a special occasion, to describe it to my friends, to wear it for the first time. Later, I bought clothes with my baby-sitting money. My first marriage was focused on the expenses of two small boys. When E-H left, I had one dress to wear job-hunting. But working, it became a pleasure again to be able to shop for clothes.

And then came Lee, and five new children, and still money enough to shop for clothes for myself. But more fun was shopping for the kids.

Six of our kids—boys and girls alike—loved to shop. But not Cheryl. She would stand in the dressing room and her sister and I would run clothes in for her to try on before she cried "Enough!"

Too soon, kids grow up and migrate and have families of their own. Buying baby clothes does nothing for me. Whether as Grandma to twelve or Mitzie to six great-grands, I had no interest in tiny clothes.

But, ah! I could hardly wait for our first little-girl offspring to turn seven, the magic age that means she's old enough to take shopping!

The fun-fest began with Jan's daughters Debbyie and Wendy. Every summer the sisters would come to visit, and we would shop till we dropped.

Jan called one evening, wanting to talk to her girls.

"Are the stores still open?" Lee replied.

"It's only 8:30, Dad," Jan said.

"Well, if the stores haven't closed yet, they aren't home," Lee told her.

Debbyie and Wendy were on a budget, but still, we took our time, loving every minute. The girls would pick things out and try them on, and I would do the unzipping and zipping and the re-hanging of the rejects.

Years passed, and other granddaughters reached the age of reason. If they lived close or could come visit in the summer, we shopped.

Of Cheryl's daughters, Kelly is like me—loving our outings together. Kacie, she's like Cheryl. Kendal rarely ever got here from New York, but when she did, we could cram quite a lot of shopping into one day.

Sally came from Montana every summer. She didn't get much wardrobe-fussing at home. Watching her tastes change was especially sweet. Frilly girl clothes. High school debating team clothes. Date dresses. I cried when I took her shopping just before she left for law school. "This is probably the last time we'll go shopping together," I said.

"Oh, Grandma," Sally said, "I promise I will come visit, all my life, and we can go shopping."

A suit for court last year. A New Year's Eve dress a few years before. It's not the same.

I took only one grandson shopping. Jan sent us with a list for Kevin's elementary school graduation. "Your mother says you need black pants, a white shirt, a tie, and a pair of shoes," I said.

"Great," Kevin said. "Let's get to it!"

"OK. Here are the neckties," I said. "What color . . . ?"

"I'll take this one," he said, picking up the nearest one.

"Kevin, that's the first one you saw!"

"It's fine. I like it."

"But . . . " I waved my arm toward three tables of ties in myriad colors and patterns.

Nope. The first one, burgundy. A reasonable choice.

He also chose the only size-12 black shoes, pulled on a

white shirt over his t-shirt to see if the sleeves were long enough, and tried on only one style of black pants.

We were finished in 20 minutes! He suggested we go see a movie.

That's not shopping! That's buying. He got that gene from Lee.

Now I have great-granddaughters! I take one girl every other summer. Lexi and I just had our third trip, and Keira would have her third next year—the absolutely most fun ever! But so was taking Kaitlyn, who just turned seven and had been talking about our shopping trip for a full year.

Watching Lexi's tastes change from choosing everything with glitter when she was seven—including a pair of blue-sequin-covered high-top tennis shoes—to "Oh, no! Not that! Nothing with glitter, Mitzie!" . . . It is so delightful.

But it's odd. I can afford to buy anything I like (within reason), yet if everything were free and I had a shopping cart, I couldn't fill it with clothes for myself. I don't much like the clothes I see.

Helping the girls pick out back-to-school clothes is better than shopping for myself ever was. Shopping for my girls, that's my annual summertime thrill.

• • •

AFTER STORY:
When my oldest great-grandson Logan turned seven, he wanted to go shopping. I thought, *This will be over quick!* But we had the same fun kind of time that I've had with my daughters, sons, granddaughters, and great-grandgirls.

Logan will get his turn every other year, just like his sister and cousins do.

The Case of the Empty Envelope
The Mysteries of the US Mail Belong in a Book.
October 5, 2015

I've always loved a mystery, from the time I first read Nancy Drew as a little girl.

Less so when I am involved in the mystery.

As part of publishing a book, marketing is involved. I recently sent a dozen books out to various places, hoping the recipients would find value in the book for their venues.

A couple weeks ago, I got back an empty envelope with "Return to sender. Attempted - not known. Unable to forward" on a bright yellow sticker at the bottom.

There was no damage to the envelope. I had used a nice envelope that made it easy to peel it opened if you didn't want to damage it. And someone had surely taken advantage of that—and sealed it back up again.

It didn't make me feel particularly good as a writer to think that my book might have been stolen.

Hmm. A strange case. I had sent all the books Priority Mail.

This one was properly addressed, destined (or not) for the OASIS less than a mile from where I live. I could have dropped it off, but it seemed more businesslike for it to arrive by mail.

I had taken the packages to the Corona del Mar post office, not much farther from me. So, that's where I started my search for what had gone wrong.

Betty, the postmaster, told me that a package doesn't go from the post office directly to a nearby address. From Corona del Mar, my book had gone to the Newport Beach post office on Camelback, and from there to Santa Ana, where everything was sorted for the carriers, before it went out for delivery back into my neck of the woods.

She ran the tracking number and said, "That's strange."

More strange stuff!?

"This package shows as 'Out for delivery.' It doesn't show that it was delivered back to you at all."

To continue the search for answers, I had to go to the Camelback office.

I arrived with an increasing collection of documents: the empty envelope, the receipt for priority mail, and the tracking information Betty had given me.

At Camelback, Kathy explained the process of "from here to there to there to here" again.

She provided me with a form to fill out to initiate a claim for repayment of postage, and, on the spot, she refunded the $5.95 I had paid.

While there, I also filled out a form initiating a search, describing the book by size and cover and colors, etc. Kathy suggested I wait a week before filling out the claim—another form she gave me—as perhaps the book would be found in Santa Ana. If not, I could seek repayment for the book.

I waited more than a week because a holiday had intervened. The book did not show up. I did not hear from the Santa Ana post office.

I filled out the claim form. At the top of it, Kathy had circled, in red, information about filing the form online. I looked at my file, which now included the envelope; the postage receipt; the tracking information; a picture of the book copied from www.amazon.com and from www.barnesandnoble.com for good measure, which showed the price; and the claim form.

I started the process to file the claim online. First I had to fill out my user name and my password. Oh, dear. I'd felt good about recording the password, but . . . user name?

The heck with that I thought. I will take this lot to the Camelback post office.

I was grateful that Kathy took charge of it all.

I wondered how many stops the package of documents would make before a check would be sent to me.

Yesterday, I received a letter from the USPS asking me to submit a description of the contents, purchase date, and cost of item. Sigh.

Sorry to report, that's as far as Nancy has come with solving this case. What became of the book will likely remain a mystery. And, possibly, what happens regarding the claim.

• • •

AFTER STORY:
The claim was declined for lack of proof that I had purchased the book. I could have filled out a half-dozen more forms, but the process had ceased to feel as if it were worth my time.

116

Bridge isn't just a game. It's THE game.
October 7, 2015

I've read that bridge is a better strategy game than chess.

Cool! I consider myself a pretty good bridge player.

I remember how upset the Times readers were when the bridge column was removed from the paper. I wrote my thanks to the editor of the Daily Pilot for continuing to print its bridge column. After a while, the Times put its bridge column back and the Pilot took its out—my point being that enough readers care about bridge that Times' subscribers get a bridge column six days a week.

Bridge can be played on several planes, so long as the plane you and your partner are playing on is at about the same altitude as your opponents'.

Otherwise, you will annoy them. And lose badly.

I play women's duplicate bridge in Encore ("old-comers" formerly Newcomers). One woman I became friends with asked if I'd like to be her partner for a duplicate group she competes in. It seemed like a nice opportunity for us to play as partners.

Lillian is still my friend, despite my humiliating myself and embarrassing her among her peers.

We arrived at about 1:00. The playing area was as big as Madison Square Garden. The bridge tables looked like a computerized quantity projected into infinity.

My confidence turned on its heel and left.

From the look of terror on my face and the fact that I was immobilized, Lillian sensed my disorientation. She has little patience with what's unreasonable to her.

"Oh, come on, Liz," she said. "We don't play all these people. We play in just a small group of them."

That enabled me to follow her to the table in the group to which we'd been assigned.

Duplicate bridge is called duplicate because all the players in a group play the same hands. A rotation system moves players and cards. If you and your partner play your hands better than the others who play them, you win.

Our group consisted of about 20 tables. In Encore, we play five tables over the course of a few hours. I looked at my watch and thought about how much I hate being in strange areas after bedtime.

In addition to bid boxes (you select your bid from a box that holds all possible bids), an electronic device sat on the table. A player enters the bid and the outcome into it, and it computes and tallies the scores. And it has a timer for play.

Lillian offered it to me to use for our team.

My fingers received jolts as if I were reaching for the ruby slippers. And I probably looked as green as the Witch. Lillian took charge.

I was on the wrong plane—in the stratosphere, without oxygen.

I remember parts of conversations, like "I'm not going to be able to do this" and Lillian saying "Yes, you are."

Playing bridge with Lee for nearly 50 years is the antithesis of playing with a new partner at the tournament level. Lillian's and my play were out of whack.

"I don't understand your bidding!" I moaned. "And I am generally quite good at defense!"

"It's OK if you don't play as well as usual, Liz," Lillian said. "You're entered as a level 1 player."

"Is there a 'level zero'?"

She ignored me.

Even the bridge gods ignored me.

And that darn timer! Hurrying is not my strong suit.

"I hate this!" I said.

"Get a grip, Liz. It's just like playing in a small group. Only bigger."

Not as I saw it.

The opponents wore green visors and dark glasses and smoked cigars, men and women alike. They came for Master Points.

"Lillian, I am totally out of my comfort zone here."

"You'll get used to it," she said.

As we moved from table to table, I held back tears. I tend to cry when lost or in danger or down the rabbit hole.

"Can't we just leave?"

"Of course we can't just leave!"

I said, "Lillian, when this is over, if I jump into your car and say 'That was fun. Let's do it again,' I want you to drive me directly to the psych ward."

One of our women opponents said, "You know, dear, some good bridge players just never become good bridge partners."

Her compassion saw me through.

When it was finally over, I couldn't believe it was still daylight.

Lillian went to check where we'd placed in the competition. I hoped they wouldn't deduct master points from her accumulation for bringing me as her partner.

"Well?" I asked. "Dead last," she said.

On the way home, I apologized for not being able to adjust to the environment. Etc.

"I get it, Liz," Lillian said. "It's not for you. I won't ask you again."

I took a deep breath for the first time in hours.

Level zero chess, anyone?

• • •

AFTERTHOUGHT:
This reminded me of decades ago when our family had a pool table. In those days, each sport I tried, I thought *This will be the one! This will be the sport I'll be good at, the one I can play without making a fool of myself.*

Only, it turned out that pool wasn't the one either.

A guest, being kind, said something about pool appearing to be a difficult game for me.

I replied, "Playing pool isn't as hard for me as thinking of something funny to say every time I muff a shot."

Treating an Indelicate Subject
as Delicately as Possible
October 17, 2015

They say that, after a certain age, a person should have a colonoscopy every five years.

All of us who have had that procedure know that it's not the procedure that we resist but the one-day preparation for it.

My lovely doctor told me there is now a new kind of test for colon cancer that is non-invasive. It is done at home, and no preparation is required. "Wow! That's for me!" I said.

It's not the polyps that are worrisome but what could be discovered that might be worse.

My doctor said the test kit would be delivered to my home. I should just follow instructions and return the kit in the enclosed packaging.

The kit arrived. It consisted of a large plastic container, a device that holds the container in a convenient place, a plastic bottle of unknown liquid, and the directions for filling and returning the container.

Oh, dear. I failed Step 1. I couldn't get the container open. It was too big for my hands, too big for my rubber lid-opener, and defiant of every method I could think of to open it. Since Lee died, I have no one to turn to for strength and discretion. Or so I first thought.

Jeanne!

When Jeanne and I were eight and seven, she was already a foot taller than I. She would surely have longer fingers!

I called her. "Hello, dearie. It's Lizzie."

"Hello, Liz," Jeanne said in that voice so dear.

"I have an awkward favor to ask of you," I said.

"Oh, Liz. What could be embarrassing between us? We have known each other forever!"

I waited a moment and plunged ahead.

"OK, well, it's this. My doctor wants me to provide a large sample of . . . fecal matter for a test for colon cancer. And I can't get the lid off the container."

When she finished laughing, Jeanne said to bring it on over.

"Thanks," I said. "On my way out to run errands, I'll drop it off. If you aren't there, I'll leave it on your porch. In a plain brown wrapper."

We shared a laugh on that.

When I went to pick up the container, Jeanne said she hadn't been able to open it either. It took her husband Merritt and all his strength to unscrew the cap.

The following day, I completed the sample according to instructions and everything was fine until the second-to-last instruction, which said to cover the specimen with the liquid in the enclosed bottle.

I looked at the specimen and I looked at the pitifully small bottle of liquid. I poured the liquid into the container. It didn't come close to covering the sample.

I thought about this for a while. I looked at the address on the packaging for shipment. I decided that by the time this got there, that liquid might well infuse the entire specimen.

I screwed the container lid back on tight and prepared it for its trip to the laboratory.

The bottom line, no pun intended, is that I passed the test. No sign of colon cancer.

My niece Kath said that, next time, I should request the container without the child-proof cap.

• • •

I'm ready to order a statement sweatshirt.
November 16, 2015

I would bet money that I get more catalogs than anyone. When I returned from being gone for six days, there were four inches of catalogs amid the accumulated mail. Add to that, an inch of assorted big post-card-type advertising offers from mortuaries, realtors, restaurants, retirement financiers, live-performance theaters, travel companies, and service vendors. Plus multiple envelopes from unknown out-of-state political candidates, charitable organizations, and others requesting contributions.

There were a few bills that made the sorting worthwhile, but basically, it was 30 pounds of wasted paper, thrown away without a second glance. Wait. I confess that I do thumb through the catalogs, but only in deference to their expense. (This is a flat-out lie. I order from catalogs all the time.)

I wondered what percentage of junk mail actually gets a positive response. [According to a Google search, a fraction of a percent.]

I do NOT want the post office to go out of business! But all this unsolicited waste? It could make an ecologist turn green.

I am in favor of mailing gifts, thank-you notes, other handwritten messages, special-occasion cards, and Christmas cards. Occasionally, I send a letter of complaint to the president of a company that has given me egregiously bad service.

About those letters regarding bad service. I am beginning to compose one to the CEO of an appliance company. About a month ago, I received an alarming letter from the company that makes my brand of dishwasher. It was a "recall notice" warning me against using my dishwasher until a defective power cord could be replaced, or it could burst into flames. I quickly called the 800 number! I was astounded to learn that they couldn't come to replace the cord for three weeks. Wow, that seemed like a long time.

Today was the day the service guy was due to arrive.

First thing this morning, I got a call from cheery Ashley saying that the repairman couldn't come today. The company had run out of replacement cords because FedEx's delivery had let them down.

Wait a minute, Ashley. The company has likely known for at least a month that there would be a big demand for replacement power cords! Seems to me the company would have a good idea of how many cords would be needed. Seems to me the cords would have been ordered *at least* concurrent with the letters going out. Seems to me there is something wrong with the upper echelon, and poor Ashley is getting the rant from the customers. She was a champ of self-composure, and I have been rescheduled ASAP—a week from now.

Daughter Cheryl has been waiting just as long for a part for her ice maker, and yesterday that service also was postponed.

I've been waiting for an escrow to close and it too was just postponed, for two weeks.

Are the planets in some funky misalignment?

I did consider ordering out of one of those catalogs. You can order sweatshirts from it with custom-made statements.

I wear a lot of sweatshirts—comfort in an array of colors. Not many of them have statements. One says "I intend to live forever. So far, so good." Most are plain or have Balboa or Newport Beach stamps or a reference to some place I've visited.

But I have an idea for a special-order statement. A navy blue sweatshirt, I think, with white letters across the front:

**WHAT IS WRONG
WITH EVERYBODY?**

• • •

"Phishers" and "scammers" and "hackers"! Oh, my!
Scammers and Phishers Prey upon Seniors.
December 1, 2015

As soon as I hear "Congratulations, you have been selected" or "You have won" or "You have qualified for," I hang up. These old tricks apparently still work on some people, despite the fact that we are expected to send $$$$ to some sleazebag before we get the trip to Hawaii, the car, or the big cash loan—as if you'd *ever* get the "prize."

My least favorite call is "We talked to your husband last year and he said you'd be interested in doing some remodeling about now." Believe me, nobody talked to my husband a year ago. This is a benign "scam"—rather, a lying sales gimmick.

In the NEW worst scam, someone calls and asks if you can *hear* her. *Do NOT say yes!* It will be nefariously construed to mean "Yes, I'll buy whatever you have to offer." Don't even say no! Because next time, NO will be the "key" word. If you feel compelled to answer, say "Who's asking?"

Every day, I hear about a new scam aimed at seniors. And occasionally, I hear about a friend or acquaintance who has fallen for a costly scam.

It's hard to be skeptical of a grandson crying on the phone about a tragedy that has befallen him and he needs money *now!* He says he has had a brush with the law—a DUI or an arrest for possession of a bit of marijuana. He promises to tell his parents as soon as he gets home, but please send him money for his bail so he isn't kept in jail in Podunk!

No! This is not your grandson. It's a scam artist.

Some recipients of calls like this are tipped off because their grandson doesn't call them Grandma or Grandpa, but Mimi or Papa or some other pet name. Either hang up or ask an authenticating question like "Did you ask your Uncle

Herbert for the money?" (This works only if it *is* your grandson and he *doesn't* have an Uncle Herbert.)

Just recently I received a call "from the US Treasury" saying this is the second time they have tried to contact me. (Actually it's about the fourth.) The spiel: I owe back taxes and if I don't call this number *now* and pay up, a warrant will be issued for my arrest.

And for the second or third time, I reported the phone number and the scam to the IRS. Just "google" IRS fraud, and you'll find a direct link. It's that common, folks!

Similar is the Jury Duty call, saying you have not appeared for jury duty, are in contempt of court, and must pay your fine right this seconde or a warrant will be issued for your arrest . . .

Don't pay them! I'm told these phone scammers demand reloadable debit cards as payment. In case you don't know, a reloadable debit card gives the holder the right to "refill" the card when the amount on it runs out. With a reloadable debit card, a scammer can empty your bank account!

Another phone scam claims to be from Microsoft. A terrible virus has been detected within your computer. Just give the caller control of your computer, follow his instructions, and it will be fixed in no time.

Don't do this! Giving access to your computer to anyone you didn't personally select enables that scuzzball to open all your files, access your social security number and bank account numbers, passwords, etc., and thereby steal your identity.

Computer-lovers like me must be particularly wary. For example, we might be used to receiving emails from our bank.

But beware. An illegitimate email can look legitimate.

I received an email from Chase Bank with the familiar Chase logo and a Chase email address, asking for my social security number. But my bank would *already* have my social security number. And, gee, that letter is grammatically slipshod . . . What's going on?

NEVER give your social security number to anyone who contacts you by email (or telephone)!! Call the institution! The fraud department will reassure you that you were right not to respond.

One email was "from Wells Fargo." I don't even have a Wells Fargo account—and yet the message says my account has been hacked. Just click on this link . . .

Don't click on the link! You can place your mouse above the link, and the true sender will be revealed. In this case, it wasn't Wells Fargo but http://alberes.com.tr/css/. I forwarded the email to Wells Fargo, and then I deleted it.

Email scams are particularly abundant. Practically everyone I know has received an email from a friend's edress saying they have been mugged in a foreign country, lost their passport and credit cards, and only you can help them—by sending them money, of course.

Don't send them the money! It's a scam.

Occasionally, an email purportedly from a friend will say just "Take a look at this website!"

Don't click on the link to the website! It won't lead to some delightful family video or photos of animals kissing each other! It *could* put a virus into your system or a worm into your computer—a passage for the unscrupulous.

Forward the email to the edress from which it came, and tell your friend her email has been compromised and to call her server.

Faster than we can recognize one fraud, "phishers" and "scammers" and "hackers" can think up new ways to separate us from our money, our identity, or our security.

As the Trojans told themselves when it was too late, and as we seniors always told our children: Be wary of strangers—whether or not they are bearing gifts!

• • •

AFTER STORY:
As I was working on the first draft of this book, I received a phone call from "Microsoft." Yeah, right.

But this was a new twist on the old gimmick. They wanted me to know that my Microsoft rights had expired, and to continue to use Microsoft Windows without interruption, I must call this phone number immediately!

If this happens to you, *don't call the number they give you!* Microsoft Windows rights do not expire.

AFTER AFTER STORY:
As I was working on what I hope is the *last* draft of this book, I got yet another scammer call. I Internet-researched the 624 area code that had displayed on my caller ID and learned that 624 is not a USA area number. It's associated *only* with telemarketers and scammers. And bill collectors trying to disguise themselves.

If you have caller ID and it shows area code 624, save yourself the irritation and don't answer the call.

The Dangers of Self-Diagnosis
December 27, 2015

My husband Lee used to say that I had a tendency to jump to "confusions."

Last Monday, I began having symptoms. I am never sick, but I had been particularly stressed lately, and I know that (worse than sugar!) stress is bad for my immune system. So after several visits to the bathroom in quick succession, off to the computer I went for some serious research!

I chose one of the medical websites that had my three main symptoms in bold print, and I scrolled to information about likely causes of the unpleasant combo. Just as I suspected, I had the stomach flu.

I read the whole article and learned that the flu can last from one to ten days, the gestation period is usually 48 hours, and after the symptoms subside, you remain contagious for up to three days. (I ignored the methods of contamination, because, well, three out of four . . .)

Three days! I had been with someone two days earlier who'd just recovered from the stomach flu! I looked at my calendar for the coming week and canceled two luncheon engagements, including one on Friday with Lillian.

After two days of unpleasantness, I dashed off an email to Lillian, whose birthday lunch I'd postponed. I said I still had severe upper abdominal pain, plus a distended stomach that made me look six months pregnant. Then I went to bed.

Wednesday morning, I awoke feeling much better. I poked at my stomach and smiled. It was over! And then I stood up and began to fall sideways. I was dizzy and clammy, and my body urged me to get to the bathroom quickly. After a bout of the worst of the symptoms, I phoned my daughter, Cheryl.

"Is this 9-1-1?" I asked her.

She chuckled. "Yeah. What's up? Are you feeling worse?"

"Much worse. I'm pretty sure I have to go to Urgent Care, or maybe Hoag. I don't want to wait an hour for the doctor's office to open."

"I'll be right there," she said. "I'm taking you to Hoag."

I threw on minimal clothing and sat at my computer to wait for Cheryl. And there was Lillian's response to my previous night's email. It said, "I really don't like your symptoms. Please go see your doctor tomorrow or to Urgent Care." Lillian is a retired nurse. I laughed at the timing but was glad to have my decision validated by my wise and knowledgeable friend.

I was admitted to a room in the ER before I had even finished filling out the paperwork.

So, it *wasn't* the flu!

But now I was pretty sure I knew what it was. About a dozen years earlier I'd had severe upper abdominal pain. I'd had an endoscopy in the ER. The official diagnosis was pre-ulcerous lesions. The doctor cauterized them, and I was in and out in no time, according to my recollection.

I asked Cheryl to notify her nearby sibs and to make it clear that, although I had been admitted to the hospital, it was no big deal. I would likely be home the next day. I also asked her to call John, our general practitioner, and he came to the ER to make his recommendations.

I was assigned a bed on the tenth floor, pre-ICU, where patients are constantly monitored. As a tech assistant rolled me through the hospital corridors, I began to sob. The last time I'd traversed these halls, just over two years ago, Lee had died.

John scheduled an appointment for the next afternoon for a surgeon to perform an endoscopy and a colonoscopy, and it turned out that I have four ulcers I didn't know about, one of which had apparently been bleeding.

I was in Hoag for four days. Cheryl made successive updates to the kids, and ultimately I had plenty of time to make phone calls (which I generally avoid, preferring wordy emails). I thanked Lillian for her advice, saying I'd read her response to my email the morning that I woke up dizzy, etc. She said, "You're lucky you woke up."

At Hoag, I was fussed over by a wonderful bunch of nurses, aides, and other staff, and watched over by John. I received ulcer med by IV, plus four units of blood and two of iron. My hemoglobin rose from 6.5 to 11.5, and John allowed me to be released a day earlier than anticipated.

What I took home from this experience—in addition to a beautiful orchid delivered during a visit by four friends—were several additions to my store of knowledge:

▸ My blood type is AB Positive. I can accept transfusions from either A or B blood-type donors.

▸ Patients should listen when someone explains patients' rights. They might need to exercise one! (I did.)

▸ Though I'll probably still jump to confusions—I should not self-diagnose.

▸ And if I'm sick for more than one day, I need to call my doctor.

You should do that, too.

• • •

Resistant to Change, Except for Some Things
Decline of Newspapers
Could Give Rise to Ignorance.
January 6, 2016

One of the best movies out now is "Spotlight," about a team of four investigative journalists who uncover decades of child abuse by the Catholic clergy. Over ten years ago, four journalists at the Boston Globe were given all the time they needed to get to the core of the scandal. Back then . . .

But with a lack of readership and falling advertising income being major issues for newspapers today, I worry.

Will newspapers continue to have teams dedicated to investigative reporting?

Will ink-and-paper newspapers go out of business?

Newspapers have taken hits because readers have easy access to online news. The younger generations are used to getting their news in bites and bits on their telephones or iPads.

We get music on iPods and on SiriusXM radio in our cars. No need for AM or FM radio with five-minute breaks for news and traffic. We don't need traffic information, our GPSes magically advise us of alternate routes due to traffic ahead.

Worse, some folks rely upon only cable news for their national and world information, but they don't know a thing about what's going on in their own neck of the woods!

We are probably the least well-informed generation since . . . well, since the days of the Pony Express.

Things change, I know. Things end. I suppose some people lamented the demise of the Pony Express.

Even though I'm 76, I think of myself as "modern" and "open minded" and "liberal." On the one hand.

But on the other hand—my dominant right hand—I am strongly resistant to change.

Before I had a chance to try a restaurant, which had replaced a long-standing favorite, it was already out of business.

The last time I went to my Hallmark store in Fashion Island to order my Christmas cards, which I had done for ten years, it was gone. Poof! I had come to know the whole family! Goodbye, Nancy and Don and Ariel! And better luck with whatever business you tackled next.

Meanwhile, there's barely a familiar store in sight.

My son Mark found a Pickwick bookmark in an old book he was taking to the library for resale. I almost cried when he showed it to me.

But who else laments the demise of Pickwick Bookstore? Bullock's, Broadway, May Company, Leeds? Probably no one.

Most people just shrug and adapt. Life goes on.

That's a good thing.

Changes in education, that's a bad thing.

When Lee started at UCLA in 1942, it cost him $29 a semester, and that included his student card, which got him into the football games.

In 1945, my mother agreed to my father's company transferring our family to California because her children would have access to California's great schools. [When we moved to Los Angeles, my father subscribed to and read both the morning Times and the evening Herald-Express.]

With current teacher layoffs in California, my son Tim, with degrees in mathematics and chemistry and a master's in education administration, can only substitute-teach. Of the tenured teachers in his county in Northern California, not one has a math or chem degree. If the district put him on full time, it would have to pay him more, and he would qualify for health care and a pension—so costly for the state. A foolish economy!

An article based on information from the National Center for Education Statistics says that, nationwide, an appallingly low percentage of science, math, and history teachers in our high schools have degrees in the subjects they teach. Search it out at www.usnews.com.

And now some universities are eliminating math requirements for admission!

Students enter college less well prepared, it takes longer for them to graduate, the cost of higher education goes higher, and grads leave college with heavy debts.

Soon, although we're one of the richest, most important countries in the civilized world, we will have only rich, well-educated but poorly informed graduates—and the biggest number of under-educated people, who *should* be educated and *should* be teaching our kids, serving coffee and fast food.

What a world.

What a quickly changing, irreversible world.

WAIT! This is a job for Superman!

Jumpin' Jehoshophat, Superman! Save the Daily Planet!

Rewind the Earth back to the way it was before all the changes for the worse in Metropolis!

(But can you spare computers and the Internet? And microwaves?)

• • •

Stress and How Not to Let it Get You Down
January 10, 2016

I know why stress is bad for us. Stress is like sandpaper rubbing on our nerve endings. Ouch! Our nerves get shorter and shorter until we run out of nerve and want to curl up like a roly-poly.

Or maybe stress is like a yo-yo that goes up and down, up and down, until the string breaks and the round thing goes shooting off into the muck and mire, and glug-glug, down we go for the last time.

Maybe people who do yoga or deep breathing or tranquilizers *have* something. Turn that stress off!

I've just gone through the most stressful month of my life. I got myself tangled into three escrows on two properties (sandpaper), with escrow dates moving backward and forward (yo-yo-ing, if you will), and I felt like just curling up and/or rolling off. Or having a bourbon and water. (As a substitute for tranquilizers?)

Why is everything so bloody complicated?

You know what sounds easy if you've never tried it? Wiring money. Somebody looks at the outgoing-money account to see if there's enough, taps on some computer keys, and whooooosh! Just like an email, the money is into the ether and will instantaneously float into the incoming-money account. Right?

What do you mean, wrong? Why does the money that leaves one account at 9:30 a.m. not land in the other account until 3:30 p.m., when it's too late to do anything with it?

So wiring money isn't direct, like the crow—or the email—flies. It's like those flocks of starlings fly, the ones that dip and swoosh in a beautiful but complicated ballet, a Sleeping Beauty of ballets (said to be the longest)—only more like several Russian ballets (said to be the longest of the longest).

Try holding *your* breath for six hours! It's stressful.

Is the stress then over? Of course not! Wired money has to go through the same thing the next day if it is relayed from one escrow to another! I'll spare you the similes. You get the idea.

But then it's over, and you've sold one property and bought another and you get the keys, right?

Wrong! Why would you think that?

The final precious document has to be recorded. I didn't ask what is involved in that, but it takes a full day, too.

And another thing, before you get that recorded deed, which will come at its own pace as a matter of course, you might get an official-looking "Recorded Deed Notice" from a rotten human being telling you that for just $83.00, he will provide you with a copy of that deed. They even have a document that shows your handwriting! (Deeds are public documents.)

This scam really bums me out because I know others fall for it. The only way these roaches get away with it is that there is so much info in so many fonts in so many boxes on this two-pager that you fail to notice the small-print disclaimer that says you don't need to pay them to get a copy of your deed, that their notice is merely a "solicitation."

Beware of that, you escrow-closers!! You've *already* paid for deed-recording and copy-receiving!

So, whatever anybody tells you about escrows and when they will close, don't believe it! Escrows are an endless piece of elastic, stretching and shrinking back, but more likely stretching and then stretching some more. Or sandpaper or yo-yos, or any other stressful thing you can think of.

Ommm.

• • •

Memories of Friendships and San Miguel de Allende
January 24th, 2016

This time last year, I was anticipating an October trip to be with classmates from high school. Planning ahead was required as the gathering would be held in San Miguel de Allende, 170 miles north of Mexico City, and would coincide with the celebration of Dia de los Muertos, All Souls Day.

Our 50th high school reunion had broken attendance records for 50th alumnae reunions at Immaculate Hearth High. Friendships renewed and new ones made, various members of the class of '57 have had many mini-reunions since then.

Many of us had also spent eight grammar school years together in big but consistent classes before four high school years in relatively small classes. We know each other pretty well. Some have maintained tight bonds since our school years, and some—like me—show up just sometimes.

Rosemary and Dolores organized the 2015 reunion. Marlene, an artist-in-residence in San Miguel, hosted us, and we enjoyed a week of delightful catching up and sight-seeing. Most of us stayed at the bougainvillea-draped Posada Carmina, a short walk from the center of town. Not much farther was Marlene's artwork-filled home, where we were regaled—when not feasting at one of the fine restaurants. It was actually a treat to walk around the town, and when we were tired, a taxi was always at hand.

I've never felt safer on a vacation than amid the celebrants in this sweet, colorful artists' village in Mexico.

The whole town dressed up for the Dia de los Muertos festivities, not just the people. Countless pastel flags—strung from the exquisite Gothic church of San Miguel Archangel to the beautiful French-style town square, El Jardín—flapped above the heads of the revelers. Around the square, villagers laid out spectacular "altars," outlined in huge marigolds and filled with sugar figurines and likenesses of their departed loved ones.

From Halloween through All Saints and All Souls days, informal parades marched up side streets to the center of town. Virtually all the participants, from babes in arms to adults, were made up and dressed elaborately, many as either Catrina—the Lady of the Dead—or her male counterpart. This might sound gory, considering Catrina is a skeleton sporting a flamboyant hat, but the stylishly-dressed skeletons and other fanciful paraders were spectacular.

Some of the participants danced in costumes so tall we thought they were on stilts, but their faces sometimes peaked out of a window of fabric in the middle of the costume.

Bands marched along or gathered in the colonnades of stores and cafes around El Jardín, playing lively Mexican music. A few donkeys, festooned in flower garlands, followed their masters. My eyes couldn't get enough—as evidenced by the numerous photos I took.

Among our touring stops were the library, the Aurora Gallery, some churches, and many shops. A trolley ride around the sights also afforded magnificent views of the town.

When my frustration level began to rise because indecision prevailed, everyone contributing their two cents, Betty reminded me of the old saying I often tell myself (and others, and then forget): "Not my circus, not my monkeys."

At Patsy's Cooking Class, we made our own lunch of pork tamales and chicken with mole sauce, and we drank hot chocolate with water and cinnamon that we stirred with a hand-carved and decorated "molinillo"—a utensil so beautiful and unique that I wanted to buy some for friends.

An answer for every souvenir desire was available in the Mercado de Artesanias. I bought a half-dozen molinillos and some attractive and inexpensive pewter trivets—a cow, pig, and donkey—what son Mark called a "menagerie à trois."

A treasure I couldn't resist followed me home, a giraffe about five feet tall—constructed of brass, pewter, and copper pieces of various sizes, made into all sorts of motifs—angels, a catcher's mitt with baseball, leaves, a slice of watermelon, an elephant, a lizard, a star, a heart. Each time I look at wonderful "Miguel," I see new figures in his puzzle-like design.

I fully appreciated the combined efforts to help purchase and ship Miguel—Betty's encouragement, Dolores' and Rosalie's translations, Pat and Phyllis and Mila's conversions from pesos to dollars and exchanges of dollars for pesos.

On our last day, Judy was faced with a lost passport, and again the women joined forces to make something happen. She would have gone to Mexico City—Ginny arranged for a driver—but Marlene thought to check on the San Miguel community website, and sure enough, someone had found the passport! We went with Judy to express our thanks to the little girl who found it and to her mother who thought to post news of it on the website.

On our last night, all of us met at the rooftop bar of the historic Rosewood Hotel to toast our farewells. As the streetlights twinkled on, we were entertained by flashes of lightning in the distance, which had also greeted us upon our arrival at León Airport.

In addition to souvenirs, delightful memories, and photos of the lovely town of San Miguel de Allende, I brought home the peaceful feeling of having been with friends. Most of us hadn't even hung out together in high school, yet we all got along as though we had been close forever.

I'll always think of this reunion as the best one ever, except, of course, for the next one.

• • •

Girl Scout Cookie Sales in the 1950s
The Citrus Avenue Girls Made Some Memories.
February 11, 2016

I got my Girl Scout cookies Sunday from my friend Carla. Well, Carla isn't a Girl Scout, she's the *good* scout who called her friends on her granddaughter Polly's behalf. Polly is the Girl Scout.

Boy, have things changed since I was a Girl Scout back in the early 1950s!

For one thing, our mothers and grandmothers didn't sell cookies to their friends. Everybody's friend *was* the mother or grandmother of a Girl Scout. Scouting was very popular then. We didn't have play dates, girls' sports, or gymnastics classes. I don't recall any of my school friends taking any kind of class outside of school. Except piano. Maybe tap dancing. And swimming.

To try to meet the unrealistic goal for cookie sales, set by someone in a Girl Scout office far away, we had to sell the cookies ourselves. I think the boxes were a dollar each and held four dozen cookies. One kind of cookie. Or maybe there were several kinds available, but my mother only bought Peanut Butter Sandwich cookies because of peanut butter being high in protein. Or maybe she liked them best.

My friends and I went door to door on the way home from our Scout meetings—in our green dresses with the yellow scarves, wearing our green berets—ringing the bell, asking whoever opened the door if they would order some cookies.

My grammar school years were filled with door-to-door canvassing.

We sold tickets for several fund-raising raffles a year, "and you don't have to be at the drawing to win the prizes."

We sold subscriptions to the Tidings, the Los Angeles diocese newspaper. I was always amazed when a housewife said she would take the Tidings. Even my mother didn't buy a Tidings subscription from me.

When we weren't selling things, we were collecting things. Paper drives were big then. It really mattered to us if our class brought in the most papers. Door to door we went, pulling somebody's little brother's Red Flyer wagon, asking if the lady of the house had any newspapers for our paper drive.

After the Fire Captain's annual visit to our school, we even went *inside people's homes*—to be certain that the people who lived along our way home didn't have fire hazards, like cords under rugs or too many plugs in one socket. If there were fire hazards, we handed out a Fire Danger Warning, and we filled out a form for school that had the name and address of the offender. Maybe they got a visit from the Fire Captain, too.

Sometimes, Jeanne and I knocked on doors, asking for the jokers from playing card decks. Collecting playing cards was a popular pastime for girls—like collecting baseball cards was for boys. You could buy blank-back cards at Kress' or Woolworth's for ten cents a pack, but your collection was more likely to be interesting if you collected from people who bought cards to play with. Lots of grownups played bridge then, and you don't need the jokers for bridge.

Didn't our mothers worry that we were accosting total strangers, asking them to buy or give us things, entering their homes?

No, they didn't. They assumed everyone was as trustworthy as they themselves.

Neighborhoods were considered safe for the people who lived in them. And neighborhoods were basically the same size as your school's district.

We went to the movies alone and trick-or-treating alone. Jeanne, Sharon, Mary Ellyn, and I—the Citrus Avenue girls—lingered in the Miracle Mile dime stores looking longingly at perfume and jewelry and makeup. Sometimes we'd wander as far as Larchmont. We walked or rode our bikes anywhere we wanted to go and were home at the time our parents were expecting us.

All that area belonged to us kids, to canvass, to explore, to loiter in, during our grammar school years.

Neighborhoods are not so safe now. Mothers in cars line up for a mile, waiting to pick their children up after school.

And grandmothers take orders for Girl Scout cookies.

Clichés become clichés because, being true, they are often repeated. So here's one that goes back to the good old days: "Oh, the good old days."

• • •

After all this time, I still miss smoking.
February 20, 2016

For the last three stressful days, I have really wanted a cigarette. It's not as if I had just quit smoking. No! I quit smoking more than 35 years ago.

But whenever I am stressed, my first thought—still—is that I want a cigarette.

Salems. That was my brand. Like inhaling Vick's Vaporub. Aaah. But this week, I'd have smoked anything if I thought I wouldn't have a major coughing fit and maybe get hooked again. I considered "vaping"—electronic cigarettes—but people look really silly smoking those. *Even* Leonardo di Caprio looks silly vaping. I saw a clip of him.

Today I was eyeing the nicotine patches at Rite-Aid, but I don't think it's the nicotine I miss.

When I was a little girl on Citrus Avenue, my father would send me to the corner Flying A gas station with two dimes to get him a pack of Philip Morris. Cigarettes from the machine cost 20 cents, but two pennies were inside the cellophane wrapper. He let me keep those.

It was during Lent ten years later when I first started smoking. I was rebellious then so rather than give something up for Lent, I decided to take up something verboten-ish.

This was almost the worst of my rebellions. Sigh. One of the bad old things about the good old days.

I had just gotten my class ring. My friends and I thought we looked SO cool! Smoking and flashing our class rings. Going to the prom and smoking. We went to Olvera Street and bought pastel cigarettes to match our prom dresses.

Every afternoon, we couldn't wait to get a mile from campus in Suzanne's old red convertible so we could light up! I burned a quarter-sized hole in my school uniform, and my mother made me iron on a patch to sort of hide it. She wouldn't replace my uniform.

I had a great summer job at Ohrbach's on Wilshire. I started my workdays in the cafeteria with coffee and a cigarette. Cigarettes from the vending machine in the employees area were 20 cents a pack (elsewhere 25 cents), and no one would say "You're under age!"

I got good grades and was accepted to UCLA, but my mother wanted me to go to a Catholic college. Mary Alice drove, and we smoked and raised our little fingers to "little people."

My all-girls college was a lot like high school and I was bored, but I learned to play bridge. Sometimes I would skip history class to play bridge and smoke in the campus Smoker.

I met a guy (who smoked Pall Malls) and dropped out of school to get married—my worst rebellion.

When I was pregnant with my first son, Tim, I sat with my OB in his office for our monthly chat. I took out my straw cigarette case. He was aghast! "What is that?" he asked. When I told him it was my cigarettes, he said, "What a relief! I thought it was soda crackers." Honest.

So, as I said, I don't think it was about the nicotine.

The phone would ring, and I'd grab my cigarettes before answering.

If anything went wrong, I'd have a cigarette while I figured out how to set it right.

Throughout my life, there were things I couldn't have, but I could always have a cigarette.

My first husband and I were poor and miserable. Cigarettes. Divorce. Cigarettes. Loneliness. Cigarettes.

I found a job. Everyone in the office smoked. Met guys, had drinks, smoked.

I met Lee. He didn't smoke, but he married me anyway. It was ten more years before I quit sneaking a couple cigarettes a day. I was 39. Lee thought I'd stopped years earlier.

But ever since, whenever there's been a crisis in my life—things not going my way—I've felt the urge to have a cigarette.

It isn't the nicotine I miss, it's the moment of setting everything else aside, sitting down, taking a deep breath (even though nicotine-polluted), watching the tip glow and the smoke curl. Getting centered.

During that time, I'd get a grip and know I could handle it, whatever *it* was. That's what I miss.

Now, of course, I know what cigarettes cost—not just the $7-something a pack, nor the coughing in the mornings, nor the reek of those who smoke, but the pain people (and their families) go through, the lives that smoking has cost.

How cool smoking used to seem. How stupid now.

I'm sure Lee saved my life by getting me to quit, but in all these years without smoking, I've never found as satisfying a way to handle stress.

• • •

AFTER STORY
My MFA friend Patricia told me her wife Cindy feels the same as I do about smoking and handling stress. She said Cindy was told that smoking reduces anxiety. I googled it, and it seems that nicotine can indeed reduce anxiety.*

Oh. So it's not just the sacred ritual.

Still, I'll never start again. My doctor told me that after 30 years, your lungs are as healthy as if they'd never encountered cigarette smoke. And I'm going on 40 years!

* To be fair, Google also had links to smoking *causing* anxiety.

I love the Internet for research! It'll back up whatever theory you have!

Is this what's meant by "dysfunctional family"?
Choose Reconciliation over Estrangement.
March 5, 2016

When I began writing this story, a saying popped into my mind: "Let the dead past bury its dead." I went online and re-discovered that the line is from Henry Wadsworth Longfellow's "A Psalm of Life." But how did it apply to what I was thinking of writing about?

Virtually everyone I know who has adult children has experienced a period of silence between the parents and one or more of their kids.

I challenge any family to match our record, avoiding the long-form details.

Lee and I were, of course, perfect parents, but over the course of our 45-year marriage, each of our seven children had an extended period of not speaking to us.

Jan, our oldest, and I had a one-year separation, 20-some years ago. For her father's birthday, he asked that we patch things up. We talked it out and have been close ever since.

Our second and fourth oldest each estranged themselves for two years once, and both of them for more than that since their father died.

The longest-term separations were between us and Cheryl and us and Mark, at seven years each.

Cheryl, our third oldest, living a great distance away at the time, trusted an ill-intentioned source. She decided her father and I were rotten human beings and we were to be ostracized until she contacted us. Seven years later, she called to say her husband's mother had died and that John was bringing her ashes to be buried alongside his father's, in Glendale.

I needed an inspired response.

"Do you think John would like Dad and me to be at the interment?" I asked. "Yes," she said. Lee and I had a lovely visit with John, and he caught us up on Cheryl and their kids. After that, Cheryl's family was back in our lives.

Mark, the youngest, was the easiest of all of our children. We had zero togetherness issues until he married the only child of a possessive family who wouldn't part with the young couple for any reason. Fortunately, in my opinion (not Mark's), his wife decided that they would be better friends than spouses, which is how we got Mark back.

The next longest separation, three years, was between us and Tim, our second to youngest. After graduating from college and going to Washington State to earn his masters in chemistry, he fell off the radar. Lee and I discussed hiring a private investigator to find him, but, out of the blue, Tim called, and—after this and that—everything turned around again.

When third-youngest Bobby married Britt, they were annoyed that Lee and I had remained friends with Bobby's former fiancée. After two years of missing them, I had a dream about a boy I used to know in grammar school, and when I awoke, I realized that if I didn't do something soon, Bobby would be "a boy I used to know." I wrote a letter and, shortly, the four of us were happy together again.

During the years of our kids' absences, Lee and I grieved and fretted about what we should do.

So what is the point?

We screw up relationships with our kids? No. A few typing errors don't ruin an entire message.

Periods of estrangement eventually end? Not sure about that one. My brother broke ties with our parents and Carolyn and me over 40 years ago.

Carolyn used to say, regarding her kids, that she could "only yodel for so long without hearing an echo."

Gosh! When I don't hear an echo, I go straight into panic mode and stay there until I can accept that not every problem is within my power to solve.

Hard to do. I know from experience.

Maybe the point is to be receptive when our kids are ready to reach out, to not rehash things . . . what Longfellow meant about "the dead past."

In that poem, he says that life just is what it is. Things aren't necessarily as they seem from *our* perspective. That we should live our lives in the present, being the best we can be, leaving "footprints on the sands of time" for others who follow.

Hard to do. I know this also from experience.

Maybe the point is that if we don't get panicky waiting to hear an echo, we might hear someone else's yodel.

• • •

What you don't know about your printer cartridges won't necessarily hurt you.
St. Patrick's Day, March 17, 2016

I think my new printer is a Republican because it is quite conservative. A few months ago, it told me I had enough black ink for only another 50 pages. Since then, I've printed hundreds of pages, maybe thousands! Writers do a lot of printing.

When I think that I've been word processing for roughly 30 years, and how I dutifully changed out old cartridges for new as notified, I get to wondering. How many of those cartridges that I responsibly returned to the manufacturer for recycling still had good months in them?

Did they get recycled as "beginner" cartridges, the ones the machines come with, which run out before you've bought the standbys?

Or does the manufacturer shake bits and bunches of unused toner into a big dispenser to fill new cartridges? Or fill the old ones to capacity and resell them to me?

I consulted the Internet. Some returned cartridges are broken down into their component parts and reassembled, replacing worn parts with new ones.

And, aha! Some cartridges are refilled—up to 15 times before they peter out! Both are sold online as "remanufactured." Buying them is discouraged for various reasons. But you can save up to 50 percent over the cost of new ones. Caveat emptor. But, man! New laser toner cartridges cost *a lot!*

Depending on the cartridge type, you can get money back for each one returned, not just benefit points from the office supply store! Did you know that some companies pay up to $22 for used cartridges? And I'd thought they were nice to supply pre-paid shipping labels! As for getting money back, all you have to do is fill out a form online, and . . .

That stopped me right there. And according to the chart, I would've gotten only $2 anyway. Heck. I could probably get more than that on the street in front of Office Depot. Savvy customers probably know there's miles of toner left.

Did you know that some manufacturers sell refills for their cartridges?

Did you know that some charities benefit from selling your used cartridges? Why do you think that is? Uh-huh.

Feeling a lot like Michael Moore, I sought out my printer manufacturer's policy. It doesn't give even the $2 the chart claimed! It does sell remanufactured stuff. I'll keep that in mind.

So what I got out of reading the manufacturer's info is that new ink cartridges are 50-70 percent recycled plastic, and new laser toner cartridges are only 10-20 percent. Some cartridges can't effectively be recycled because the cost of recycling exceeds the savings in raw product. It can take a thousand years for the parts to decompose.

This is bad. I now feel greedy and *guilty*. I want my printed drafts, *and* I am a contributor to landfill abuse.

Thank goodness for those who sell refilled cartridges on the black market! I mean *online*.

Considering that (from what I read) a typical toner cartridge has a life of only 2,000 pages and I've gotten that many since I was warned mine had only 50 pages left . . . I'll bite the bullet and buy new. And I won't begrudge my printer's manufacturer the opportunity to recycle my cartridges, however they benefit.

But not before I know they're really, truly empty.

• • •

In my mind, it's the best invention ever.
**An Old-fashioned Girl with a Camera
Easter Sunday, March 27, 2016**

What do you think is the best invention ever?

What first might come to mind is the wheel. Or sliced bread (*that* sets the bar pretty low). But I am talking about the best invention of modern times, for you, personally. Not world shaking things like television, the computer, the Internet, airplanes, or even the smart phone, although your personal favoritism might start and stop with one of those.

You'd think my favorite would be electronic word processing, but it isn't. Although it sure beats my parents' old Underwood!

For a while recently, I said the two best inventions of modern times were the GPS and the DVR—definitely excellent conveniences.

My mother, in her "modern times" in the 1950s, said the permanent wave was the best invention. She said that despite having to sit hooked up to a medieval-looking torture device with electrically wired clamps attached to the curlers that heated the chemicals and set the permanent wave. You'd think her fave would have been the electric washing machine.

In my sister's modern times, she thought the Selectric typewriter was the invention to end all inventions. Eventually Carolyn converted to a Mac, leaving 35 bankers boxes of poetry among—as she called them—her "*wordy* goods."

But back in our childhood—when we both had been subjected to the barbaric beauty-parlor wave—Carolyn thought the cold wave was the best invention. My sister was beyond perming her hair when she was in high school, but she had the patience to give both my mother and me our Toni perms.

What a smelly mess! Tight curlers, chemical solution dripping into my eyes and down my neck, and Mother asserting that "It takes pains to be beautiful." Beautiful?

The photograph of me in grammar school with the tight, uncombable ringlets is etched in my memory.

And that leads to *my* all-time favorite invention, the camera. I thought my first Brownie box camera was the most precious thing any kid could own. The black-and-white negatives were the size of the photo (eight to a roll of film), so the pictures were crisp and clear.

For years, my father stuck with his accordion Kodak with the push button at the end of a cable. My mother would send pictures to her mother and sisters in Chicago, and in due time they would be returned and then attached with little black corners to the pages of the family photo album—pics of our 1950 Buick with Dynaflo, my sister's graduation with me wearing her mortar board, my brother in his Air Force uniform, my parents in front of the first house they owned.

When I think of my family, I don't bring their faces to mind. I bring to mind their faces in the *photos* they were in, in the times I'm remembering. Like Daddy with Mother seated on the bicycle I got for Christmas the year I turned 12. I've looked at the old photos so many times that photo-memories have replaced the real people in my mind's eye.

I am an inveterate recorder of family events. Our family accumulated over 30 photo albums. The grandkids loved to page through them to see what their parents looked like at their ages, and the newest generation can see what their mothers, their grandmother, and their great-grandmother looked like when they were young.

I think of family occasions, and there we all are, in my head, our children, our grandchildren, and now our great-grandchildren.

I never went on a trip without documenting every sight (another 30-plus albums), usually with my husband Lee in the middle of the picture. Now that he's gone, I think of a trip, and there's Lee, in my inner vision, in front of Le Mont St. Michel, atop St. Peter's in Rome, or on the Great Wall of China.

Taking pictures has become a breeze compared with our earliest travel days when Lee carried all the apparatus for me. With my digital camera, I don't have to have dozens of rolls of film processed. Now I take thousands of photos on a disk smaller than a quarter, and I can decide which pictures to have printed.

I resist using the cell phone that my kids made me get. And I still read real books, too. I'll never take to an electronic reader.

I'm just an old-fashioned girl, with a modern camera.

. ● .

To predict, or not? That is the question.
April 24, 2016

Like most folks, I read the daily horoscope—you know, on my way to the bridge column. It's comforting to realize that one-twelfth of all the people in the world should need the same advice as I on the same day as I.

If horoscopes would advise when to jump in bed, cover our head, and not get up till the morning, a lot of frustration might be spared us.

How far in advance can astrology reach? Or are some days unpredictably ill-fated?

My BFF Marian and I planned months ago for me to visit her in March. A year has passed since she moved to Las Vegas to be near family, and we were long overdue for visiting.

If I were skilled in the arts of astrology, would I be able to predict a better time for visiting? Or would I pull out my charts, take up my compass, check the alignments of the planets, and plot the most perfect week—for everything to go wrong?

I made plans. My tickets were in order. A shuttle at my auto dealer's hub would take me to the airport and pick me up upon my return. and while I was gone, my car would be serviced, and I would have new tires, according to my explicit instructions.

All I had to do was arrive at the hub 40 minutes before I needed to be at the airport.

The morning of the flight, I was fully prepared. I was almost fully prepared. I entered the destination into my GPS and headed up Bristol. I made the U-turn at Birch, and the GPS said, "You have reached your destination."

What? Where? A Burger King? A car rental agency? I saw nothing that said the name of the dealership.

Around the block I went. This is not an ordinary city block. The streets were designed to keep traffic *out* of the residential neighborhood. They're further disrupted by a freeway.

By the second time around, I was crying. I was supposed to have arrived 15 minutes earlier! Fortunately the dealership itself was not far from where the hub should have been, so I drove there.

"Help me! Help me!" I sobbed, not at all like a strong Disney heroine.

Ten minutes later I'd followed an employee to a tiny building on Bristol with a classy, low-impact sign on its front, nothing that would catch the eye of a first-timer.

Eventually I stopped crying and my flight and I left.

I settled in to read my paperback, which I'd selected from my stack of new books. I soon realized that I'd already read the book, some period of time before a friend's recommendation inspired me to buy it (again).

I would buy a different book in San Francisco (anything to avoid leaving from LAX).

After a change of planes at SFO, I arrived in Las Vegas. The only other time I'd flown into McClarran Airport was in the 1970s. Such a sweet airport—like Lockheed-Burbank used to be.

Holy Nellie! McClarran's as big as LAX now!

I called Marian and told her the number of the baggage carousel where I was waiting, not realizing I should also have told her which terminal. While I waited, I continued reading the second inadvertently-already-read book of my trip.

An hour passed before Marian found me. (I'd turned my phone off to save the juice to call the shuttle upon my return.)

Mar and I enjoyed an evening of chatting, feasting on crackers and cheese and veggies and an entire bottle of a very nice pinot noir. We spent the next day of our three-day visit in our jammies, catching up. It was heaven!

Then I spent the night throwing up. On the way to Urgent Care the next morning, I tripped in Marian's garage and landed face-plant style. It took a while to find the Urgent Care, where I got a shot for "the little flu" that's going around.

Yeah. Around airports!

The rest of my visit I lay on Mar's couch, consuming tea and chicken soup while we overdosed on political coverage.

Oh, sweet SNA airport! Oh, sweet shuttle! Oh, sweet service department! But wait! No new tires.

Something to deal with after the weekend.

Once home, I looked at back issues of the Times, saved by my neighbor Suzy, to see if the Pilot had published my story. (It had!) Next I read the back horoscopes to see if there'd been a warning that this hadn't been a favorable time for me to go visiting. (No such sign.)

The next day I tended to the things that had accumulated while I was away. I entered the monthly payables in Quicken and pulled out the printer's paper drawer to place the checks in it. Oops, too fast. The drawer fell out. And I couldn't get it back in.

I got the flashlight to see what was in the way of the drawer, seeing nothing. I opened the compartment to the toner cartridges, which also provided no useful information. And then I couldn't close the door to the cartridges.

It's a new week. I made an appointment to get the tires, and Brian should be here early this afternoon to reassemble the printer.

Marian now has the "little flu." If not for us finding the Urgent Care so she herself could now make use of it, I'd think the Universe was being downright peevish.

• • •

How to Avoid the Bucket List in the Sky
April 17, 2016

When someone dies, it's almost as if the person got checked off of a bucket list. God's "Take-to-Heaven" list, maybe.

We don't tend to put dying on our bucket lists—the point of a bucket list is to name what we want to do before we die. Climb Mount Everest. Go sky-diving. Swim nude in Lake Cuomo. None of those is on my list.

Sometimes I feel as if I'm squandering the last decades of my life. I argue with myself about that.

"You should be doing something important, not just thinking about it!" That voice sounds something like my mother's.

"Wait a minute," I respond, "I've already done important things! I've raised a heap o' children. Some of them even like me!

"I've also educated myself, worked to support my family's welfare, and contributed to worthy causes.

"I've been a good citizen.

"I've volunteered, albeit to do something I like doing.

"Aren't those things important?" That voice sounds like Lee's. His doesn't sound whiney like mine.

And yet I worry that I'm not using my allotted time well. Should there be more stuff on my bucket list?

If you've checked everything off your list, it doesn't mean you're ready to die. It just means you're content.

I've been everywhere I really wanted to go. Some places I'd like to visit again, but I don't feel compelled to put them on a to-do list.

I don't want to do noble things. I want to donate money so that *other* people can do noble things.

I want to laugh and try to make other people laugh. I

want to hug people and make them feel good about themselves. I want to play Spider solitaire on the computer.

OK, Mother. I know what you're thinking. That I spend too much time on the computer. And you've probably recently heard, in your corner of heaven, that sitting is the new smoking.

So, OK, I've started doing what I would never put on my bucket list or even on my New Year's Resolutions list. I've started walking again. I used to walk six mornings a week, for years. Lee and I used to walk together, and when he couldn't do that anymore, I'd get it out of the way as soon as I awoke so we could have our days free.

Then my hip started to bother me. When that was better, my knee started to bother me. Then it was too cold, Or hot.

Then Lee got checked off of that bucket list in the sky, and that was my excuse to just sit and do little. Well, I did write a book, and I do write stories that I hope someone will publish. I also read. And I manage to play bridge once a month—instead of the six times Lee and I played.

But all in all, I do nothing, and I have no excuse.

That "Sitting is the new smoking" thing motivated me. Besides being good for one's heart and bones and general well-being, I recently read that exercise is now said to be very good for our aging brains! I see videos of seniors doing line dancing, and I hear my mother's voice. "Well?" she says.

So I'm walking—and exercising my brain at the same time. I started small, just around my block. Gosh, I used to walk all the way to the furthest reaches of our community and back.

How things have changed. It broke my heart to discover that in our community's effort to decrease our water usage, the landscape committee decided to cut down the trees in the green belt. There were bird houses there for sweet little blue birds to nest! I've never seen that bird anywhere else. And do existing trees actually take much water to maintain? My gardener says they don't.

I suppose when I get used to the changes, I'll go back to appreciating the song of the birds who still find places around here to nest, the sight of bunnies hopping to their hiding places, and the smell of the newly mown grass in our greatly reduced greenbelts.

And finding fault with the landscape contractors who seem to have no forethought regarding how to space drought-resistant plants in a practical arrangement. When these closely-bunched babies reach full size, they'll interlock, and a *whole lot* of water will evaporate in the tops of the plants and never get to the roots.

Yes, I spend part of my walking time criticizing good people who volunteer to do the work required to keep a homeowner's association running—one of those important things that I don't do. So shoot me.

Plus avoiding over-friendly dogs and eyeing the dog-walkers to be sure they scoop up their dogs' poop. . . and don't put it in my trash can.

And wondering which of my neighbors is so intent upon smashing snails on the walkway where they dry out and stick.

Generally just being crusty old me, although a healthier version of me. A long way from being checked off.

. . .

There was an old(er) woman who couldn't say no.
Theme Parks Haven't Changed Much,
but My Center of Gravity Has.
April 30, 2016

We're never too old to stop learning. About stuff, about life, about ourselves.

Son Mark and I just returned from what the time-challenged call a "stay-cation"—ours, five days of sensory overload at theme parks and movie studios.

If on a recent trip to Disneyland you saw a woman in her senior years being hauled out of a boat from the Pirates of the Caribbean by two burley men and a forklift, that was I.

Disneyland hasn't changed much in 20 years—except for adding a phenomenal light show—but I seem to have changed a lot. Oh, the aching muscles and stiff joints! Oh, the elongated distances between two points! Oh, the exhaustion! Oh, the shift in location of my center of gravity! I refuse to blame the discomforts on age, but rather on disuse of body parts.

And I changed out hearing aid batteries twice. I thought I'd bought a faulty package of 312s until I realized the self-adjusting aids had been compensating for the clackety tracks, the blaring music, and the joyous screams of revelers.

In fairness, it's not all Disneyland's fault.

It's Universal Studios' fault, too.

Before Lee died, he'd told Mark, "If your mother wants to go somewhere, go with her." Mark's involuntary liberation (divorce) allows him to honor Lee's request.

We thought we'd go to Orlando this year, but fortunately the Harry Potter/Hogsmeade exhibit opened at Universal Studios in Hollywood in time to save us the plane fare.

Besides visiting Universal's wondrous Wizarding World of Harry Potter (a magical story in itself), we went to Paramount and Warners', and Disneyland and California Adventure.

Adventure? I'm a sedentary woman of 77. Mark, much like me although of course younger, got a strong dose of what's ahead as he helped me into and out of cars, trams, and roller coasters.

Twenty-ish years ago, I went on the last great wooden roller coaster, the Colossus at Six Flags Magic Mountain, with granddaughter Sally. I figuratively kissed the ground when I alighted, swearing that *that* would be the last big roller coaster I would ever ride.

It's weird to be of an age to speak in decades, but for three of them I'd been the "fun" parent/grandma—the one who rode roller coasters with the dauntless among our offspring.

After the Colossus, I became more like their prudent parent/grandpa with the good sense to avoid terror and danger. Yet, on the last day of our stay-cation, Mark coaxed me into riding the Adventure park's California Screamin'.

Screamin'? I was stark silent with eyes squeezed shut. As evidenced by the photo, taken at a point I will never know, my mouth is a clenched slit, my hair is blown straight up like a Troll Doll, and my knuckles are as white as skeleton bones. [See cover.] Never again. No more scary rides!

Maybe no more theme parks. . . . She said.

There are a half-dozen great-grands now, and I noticed that many elder theme park junkies ride to the front of the line in wheel chairs and electric go-carts—with their entire parties.

Yes, I've changed. But, my memory of discomfort is quick to fade. And what hasn't changed is that, when it comes to having fun, it is beyond difficult for me to say no.

• • •

Embracing the Magic at My Fingertips
The Wizarding World Enchants Adults Too.
May 11, 2016

My mother let us read comic books. Part of our weekly allowance was allotted toward a 10-cent "Archie" or "Superman."

Dr. Feehan, our pediatrician, told her the best thing she could do was get us interested in reading, regardless of what we wanted to read. (He might be more circumspect these days.)

Mother read to us, mostly from volumes of "My Bookhouse" and "My Travelship." My sister Carolyn and I progressed naturally from storybooks and the funnies in the newspaper to borrowing library books and to purchasing our own books, and ultimately to writing them—although Carolyn wrote poetry.

My days of reading nightly to children had passed before J. K. Rowling emerged in the mid-1990s. But news of a young woman writer and her stories about a boy wizard's fantastical experiences intrigued me. I read my first Harry Potter book, and I was hooked.

Each successive volume arrived from Barnes & Noble on its publication date. I loaned the books to my son Mark and I told my grandkids about them, getting parental permission before giving Potter books as gifts to the littlies.

My sister Carolyn, some of her offspring, Mark, and many of my grandkids became enthusiasts.

I wept throughout the first movie because, being a writer, I was overcome with emotion seeing Rowling's imagination become "reality."

I longed to go to Orlando and see the stories' settings in life-size, substantive 3D. And then—*Accio!* The Wizarding World of Harry Potter opened at Universal Hollywood, in our own back yard!

Buying our tickets months in advance, Mark and I could hardly wait to enter Hogsmeade!

Of all the theme parks I've visited, Wizarding World is the most fanciful! Even a mature woman can become enchanted.

Beginning and ending our day at Universal in Hogsmeade, Mark and I thought we'd enjoyed every inch of its sights and shops, but as we were about to leave, we noticed a crowd in front of Ollivander's Wand Shop.

What could it be?

The line moved at about twenty-five wanna-be witches and wizards every fifteen minutes. Mark got us some butterbeer, and we settled in to people-watch for half an hour.

Frankly, I welcomed the recovery time. Theme parks are exhausting for adults who don't run marathons.

Behind us in line were two young brothers and their parents and grandparents. The glow of amazement and joy on the boys' faces reminded me of young Mark and Tim when they first visited Disneyland.

The brothers became restless standing and waiting. Their father, concerned that we might dislike having our handrail/ leaning post joggled, spoke sternly with them, and then he left.

I felt bad for the kids. Come on! I'd been parentally chastised in public in my youth. It's humiliating, and you feel like all the fun you've been having has been snatched away.

Mark and I engaged the boys in cheery chitchat. Tristan and Damon were 11 and 8 years old. Their mother was reading them the fifth book in the Potter series.

Their grandmother had been a teacher for 35 years. She said she'd read some of the first Potter book to her class, but a parent found out and complained to the principal.

How counter-productive! In the third grade, Sister Loretta read our rapt class "A Secret Garden," and I passed along the book—and love of reading?—to my grandkids.

Books connect generations.

The family was nice and our conversation lively.

Damon said, "It's ironic, but Tristan who hates snakes, wants to be in Slytherin House!"

Mark told him he was impressed that, at only 8 years old, Damon knew how to use the word "ironic" correctly.

You know how it is when you connect with strangers, even for as little as half an hour, and you just feel better for it? It was like that.

Soon we were inside Ollivander's. Tristan and Damon were the only young children in our crowd and were invited to the front for the demonstration. We big kids stood near the walls of the small shop. The lights were dim, and only the brothers' sweet faces were lighted—like a picture on a Christmas card, revealing all the trust and wonder of youngsters.

The Wand Lady—"Call me 'The Wand Lady,'" she'd said—made thoughtful selections from seemingly endless stacks of beautifully boxed wands.

As each boy tried out his wand, the wrong thing happened. Instead of a bell ringing once, it rang repeatedly. Instead of a box flying from the shelf, the whole storecase buckled.

"Oh, no!" she said. "The wands made their choice, but I see that I've placed them backwards. This one is for *you*, Tristan. *This* one is for you, Damon."

I was sorry for the demonstration to be over. The boys were unconditionally "in the moment." They were wizards! How awful it would be if they couldn't have their interactive wands! I wanted that moment to continue! (I know, I know.)

Before anything was etched in stone, I whispered into

the mother's ear, "Would you allow me to buy the wands for your sons?"

The mother looked at me for a moment, as if deciding whether I was a sorceress or a Muggle. "Are you sure?" she asked.

"I would love to! I couldn't've done that when my boys were little, and it would mean so much to me if you would let me do it for your sons!"

Tristan and Damon were thrilled, of course, and as surprised as if I'd exclaimed *"Waddiwasi!"* and all the wands had started flying through the air.

The boys and their mother and grandparents gave me their thanks and hugs, and several of us had tears in our eyes.

Mark told me that before I'd spoken to the mother, he thought he'd heard her say, "You can have your pictures taken with the wands, but . . ."

I watched the boys later, at several of Hogsmeade's interactive windows, reciting incantations and waving their wands to make lamps light and boxes open.

Magical.

• • •

AUTHOR'S NOTE:
In case you thought I'd given the boys fanciful names for their anonymity in the newspaper, their real names were Griffin and Phoenix.

I dreamed that I stopped getting unwanted calls.
Realtors Are a Persistent Lot,
Even When You Don't Want to Buy or Sell.
June 15, 2016

I just read on the Internet—so it must be true—that if you dream that your teeth are falling out, it means that you've said something unkind that you regret. Oh, dear. I do dream from time to time that my teeth are crumbling and falling out.

But me? Say something unkind?

It's those darn realtors, isn't it. I try to tell them nicely that I don't want to sell my house or buy an apartment building, but one company in particular—M&M Pesterers, I'll call it—has 1200 salesmen and all but 200 of them have called me since Lee died.

I was nice with the first 300 or so. I explained that my husband used to be willing to spend his afternoons teaching them about real estate, but that I have no interest in spending my time that way. I tell them that if I wanted to buy or sell, I'd call the broker Lee and I have used for over 25 years.

Lee taught *him* a lot, too, and getting advice from Marty is about the same as being able to ask Lee directly.

But nothing nice I say to realtors stops them. My blood pressure rises as, despite each kind word, they refuse to give up. When I flat out say they're wasting their time, they promise they'll take my name off their list—but that doesn't affect the M&M master list, available to all their other salespeople.

And you likely know that anybody with a list sells it to someone else, and you're helplessly on about a zillion lists except the one that might matter, a functioning "Do not call" list.

You can forget about the "Do not call" list you signed up for. One caller acknowledged that they don't check names on the lists they've bought against the "Do not call" list.

Most people think the list covers all phone solicitations except for charitable donations, but the "Do not call" list only applies to *interstate* calls. Calls that originate within your state are not covered by the "Do not call" list. Your neighborhood caller *might* be intimidated if you tell him you're on the list—if they're not aware that to stop local callers you have to keep a record of the offenders' phone numbers and report them to the State Attorney General.

You can record the phone numbers and block them through your phone company. They still call, but the readout on the phone tells you it's a blocked number.

You can also say, "It's illegal to solicit someone whose spouse has died." That scares the one who started his pitch with "I talked to your husband last year and he said you might be ready to do some painting about now."

Believe me, bub, you didn't talk to my husband last year.

Someone told me to say, "You're on the air, caller. What is your experience of Rastafarianism?" Or some such.

I have come to not answer any calls if I don't recognize the readout, but some sneak through. Mostly, phone solicitors don't leave messages, which is nice of them. But lots do.

I get about one personal call to every five sales calls. A solicitor told me to say that I rent so I'm not the one who hires (1) home remodelers, (2) handymen, (3) solar panel installers, etc.

You understand. You probably get as many unwanted calls as I do. Except from realtors.

Last Sunday, at two in the afternoon, an M&M Pesterer called. Mostly, when the readout tells me it's M&M, I just don't answer.

But I answered this call. "Honestly? M&M is calling me on Sunday afternoon to try to get me to buy or sell something? You and cockroaches will survive a nuclear blast! I've told hundreds of you who have called that I don't want to talk to you!"

"I like you, Mary," the agent said. "I wouldn't have called on Sunday, but I've been unable to reach you during the week."

I rolled my eyes for two reasons. First, he was probably right since I generally ignore M&M calls. Second, I hate it when someone who doesn't know me calls me by my legal name.

"You don't know me well enough to call me Mary," I said. "Well, uh, Ms. Newman, uh, . . . "

"Look, I am just an old widow lady with a house I love and all the property I need, and I want to be left alone."

"But how do you know what you need if you don't keep in touch with the market?"

"I—have—all—I—want."

"But I have this sweet 12-unit building . . . "

I interrupted him. "We're at the point where either you say, 'Thank you for your time. I'm sorry I disturbed you' or I just hang up on you."

"Well, then, both."

Both? "OK, I'm hanging up. Don't call back. Ever."

Come to think of it, I won't dream about losing my teeth tonight, because I don't regret what I said.

What I regret is not just saying "M&M, huh." And THEN hanging up.

• • •

REMINDER:
The 624 "area code" is associated *only* with telemarketers, scammers, and other undesirables. If your caller ID shows area code 624, don't bother to answer the call!

Seeing the World Through Colored Filters
Examining Life's Unfiltered Comments
July 1, 2016

When I was a little girl, I would occasionally get a piece of hard candy wrapped in colored cellophane. I was as delighted with the colored wrapper as I was with the candy. I loved looking through the yellow or red or green paper and seeing my world in a different light. I used to save the little squares of color.

In high school, the song "La Vie en Rose" was popular, and Sister Gemma gave our French class the words to the song. I still remember them. What they say is that the emotions of love color our world in a softer, sweeter, rosier light.

When I was in my thirties, I took photography classes, and I had all the paraphernalia that went with clunky cameras and long lenses. A yellow lens on top of the regular one made black-and-white outdoors pictures much sharper.

Anything between us and our natural vision is a filter. But they're not our only filters. Internal filters prevent us from saying something to get us in trouble or to hurt someone else's feelings.

To use this meaning in a sentence, I've heard it said that Donald Trump has no filters. But this isn't about him. It's about a relative of mine, my cousin-in-law Slim.

Ever since Slim married my cousin, I have been encouraging everyone to cut the poor soul some slack because it's hard to come into a big family, and it's hard to do this, and it's hard to do that. I have been Slim's biggest supporter.

We're going to have a family reunion. I sent email invitations to all the relatives, saying that, to keep things simple, I would contact only one person in each family.

When I hadn't heard from my cousin, even after three emails about the event, I wrote Slim.

In return, I got a lengthy email listing years of my slights, oversights, mis-speaks, and other perceived misdeeds. Honestly, I couldn't remember some of the things, and some of them I couldn't believe anyone could find fault with.

Yes, sometimes I can be unkind. But I usually choose those times and those people with full clarity and aforethought. Like when I told an acquaintance that she was unquestionably the most unpleasant person I ever met.

Hey! I'm not claiming *my* filters always work.

I don't expect others to be perfect either. And (I know, I know) sometimes they have issues we know nothing about.

All the same, it came as a surprise that Slim had long been compiling a list of my failings. She let loose that list with a verbal Gatling gun, adding that they wouldn't be attending the party.

Oucha magoucha! Most of us would have just said, "Sorry, we're busy that day."

Some slices of life don't strike you funny, or make you feel good—or bad. They just make you think.

I think most of us either have genetic filters or we're super-cautious not to hurt anyone's feelings because that's what our mothers or the nuns taught us when we were kids.

But I've often thought that our innate reticence to say what we're thinking gives other people permission to blurt their vitriol willy-nilly, knowing that we won't respond in kind.

Some people would say "no holds barred" and some might say "with the gloves on" (or off, whichever is worse). I say it's done without filters.

Or, maybe through a treasured square of black cellophane.

• • •

Oh, look! A chicken!
Politics Might Be the Link to Adult-onset Add.
July 7, 2016

Son Mark was one of the first generation of kids to be diagnosed as "hyperkinetic." Clearly, he got a bad hand-me-down gene from his father's side of the family.

In the late 1960s, hyperkinesis was the diagnosis for easily distracted kids who couldn't sit still and focus on their schoolwork. Later it became known as ADD—Attention Deficit Disorder.

My family had no signs of behavioral problems. We were all high achievers, getting good grades and never causing trouble. OK, I got my worst grades in Conduct or Deportment, depending on the school. But I always finished my work before others and needed someone to whisper with.

What kids can sit with their hands folded on their desks and just *wait* for the slower learners? The nuns should have let us do crossword puzzles.

I've long thought of myself as an efficient juggler of tasks. There's an email that goes around that speaks of getting older as going into one room to find one thing and being distracted by something else that sends you into another room where you get sidetracked by something else, ad infinitum, until nothing gets finished and the first step is utterly forgotten.

Not me. I'm pretty good at getting that first task done—in fact all the tasks done—just not necessarily of a piece.

For instance, this morning I sat down to breakfast, and I read an article in the Times that, before I forgot, I just had to email to several family members and friends, after which I started to play a game of Spider solitaire, before I remembered I was in the middle of my protein bar and fruit compote.

Breakfast finished, I went to work on my new book about what it means to get your affairs in order ("Rest Assured"), but I decided I really needed to write my grandkids because Jan had said that some of them were planning not to vote—as a political statement of disassociation from the process and disregard for both candidates. So I ended up writing everybody I know an email about how important it is to vote, and then I went back to work on my book, which mentions property deeds and never to dispose of them.

And I remembered that my daughter Cheryl told me the house her family lived in before her parents' divorce was vacant and in a shambles and last sold at auction for a fourth of its "location, location, location" value because title couldn't be established. So I went to zillow.com, copied its sales history and emailed my property manager to ask how a title could have become so complicated since 2013 that it couldn't be safely purchased.

Then I went back to writing my book, and I realized that one of my own affairs wasn't in good order so after I wrote an email about that, I noticed that replies to my email about voting had started to come in, and one was from Carol, my high shcool alumnae director, which made me stop to check whether I'd updated my class of '57 roster lately because our 60th reunion is next year, and would it be cheaper to hold the reunion at school or at Diane's? (I'm unofficial everlasting class secretary.)

Thinking of where it would be better to put the reunion money made me think to email Cheryl that if she contributes to the national party, her money could be put into the presidential campaign rather than the Senate or House campaigns.

Cheryl thinks that, like Mark, she had ADD as a kid and still does, and although she isn't really related to me by blood, I joked in that email that I'd been pretty distracted all morning and maybe she and Mark *do* get their ADD from me.

And then I thought about those email seniors and wondered if ADD could be acquired in later life, and I researched it on the Internet, and it can be!

And that's when I got the idea for this article. ADD is of common interest and I'd start with how Mark got it from his patrilineal side—no symptoms on the maternal side—and I'd like to finish this piece, but I need to get back to my . . .

Oh, look! A crow is walking on the wall outside my window!

• • •

SIDE STORY:
Speaking of crows . . .

Other people notice things about us before we do. I remember Jeanne saying, when we were Christmas Company shopping together, "Liz, you are distracted by every shiny thing you see! You are just like a crow!"

I love shiny things! I didn't know I was akin to crows!

But, in case you didn't know, I can be distracted by things that aren't shiny.

New Phone System Calls up Old Phone Memories.
Remembering the Days
When Phones Weren't So Smart
July 28, 2016

Remember when all you had to do to use a phone was plug one end of a flat cord into it and the other into the phone jack, then connect the handset to the phone with a long curly cord so you could dial a number, and then walk all over the house and talk?

I remember when black fabric-covered cords were "hard wired" to the wall and the handset alone weighed about ten pounds. The round dial went pssssht when you inserted your index finger in the hole by the number and moved it to the curved finger-stop, and then click-click-click-click-click as the dial returned. Now that's "dialing"!

The first phone number I remember—probably because I'd become old enough to call friends, plus it was typed in the circle in the middle of the dial—was WHitney 7165. You dialed WH 7165. My Citrus Avenue friends had other prefixes. Mary's was WYoming, and Sharon's and Jeanne's were WEbster. The three of them had five numbers, not just four like ours.

In 1962, my phone number was WEbster 8-3000, and it was fun to say it was the same as how many hot dogs Webster ate at the baseball game.

Phone numbers changed in the late 1960s when I lived in the San Fernando Valley. My number went from DIckens 3-3143 to 343-3143. That was my number when Lee and I were dating. Ah, sweet memories. Before area codes.

I had five mismatched stationary phones in my modest-sized home, but I've yielded and replaced them all with portable phones. My friend Ruth's husband John talked me into it a couple weeks ago after I'd ranted about all my unwanted callers. John said he'd bought a telephone system (I didn't even know what a telephone system was) *with a button that blocks calls.*

Whoopee! It was like promising me heaven in a box.

Installing the new phones was daunting. I expected as much when the top of the box included instructions for how to repackage the contents. It was another unpleasant introduction to the world as the *rest* of humanity accepts that it works . . . Well, those who communicate with the rectangular smudged-up glassy things that are always within their reach.

Did you know that a man recently married his cell phone in Las Vegas, with his wedding ring attached to "the bride"? A natural evolution of such single-minded devotion.

I have a cell phone. It's my second. My first had a lifetime $20 contract and was never charged when I wanted to use it. My kids insisted I get a smart phone. Now I have a cell phone that is never charged that costs me $70+ a month. Since I learned to slide my finger over it to turn off the power, it stays charged longer, but the extra $50 a month has not enhanced my life.

My kids' phones chime or chirp or bark or play symphonies when they get a call. In fact, I don't remember what mine does because it's always off. I've told everyone that all my phone does is dial out, and only 9-1-1.

Maybe it's because I don't get cell calls that I have a negative reflex when someone I'm with must answer calls, texts, and whatever else makes cell phones indispensable for even the amount of time it takes to eat lunch. My family can reduce an entire Thanksgiving buffet to leftovers in ten minutes.

The first time I was in a restaurant and someone was using a cell phone in a rather loud voice (probably to show off that he had a cell phone)—silly me—I asked if he could wait until he left the restaurant to finish his call.

Offended, he said, "I'm doing business here!"

Offended, I replied, "We're having dinner here! It's a restaurant, not an office! "

WHitney 7165 was never answered at dinner time. And the ball was still in the caller's court because there weren't message machines then. People just called back later, and they called back if the line was busy. (Cox, my phone company, won't let me have a busy signal, and I still don't know what to do with the person I'm talking to when the phone pings an incoming call.)

I do recognize the value of cell phones. They are especially good for parents of young children. They make it possible for business people to receive calls when away from the office. And they're handy if you're trying to find someone at the airport, assuming I'm not the person you're trying to find.

But, come on, folks! Don't be tethered! Your cell phone is not attached to the ring finger of *your* left hand!

Come to think of it, the only places phones don't ring (or aren't supposed to) are theaters, libraries, and bridge-game rooms. No wonder I love movies, books, and bridge!

So my new phones—which are as light as marshmallows but required the moving of heavy furniture to plug in their remote bases—they're ready! I can't wait to block a realtor's call.

If only I had a block button on the mailbox. The trees we'd save!

• • •

AFTER STORY:

I tried to block a call to my land-line the other day, and the phone lit up to tell me the call-block memory was full.

I looked in the Operating Instructions to find out how many calls could be blocked. The answer: 250.

In less than a year, I'd blocked 250 realtors, home remodelers, scam artists, and other undesirable chat-mates.

Yessss!

But now what?

Changes to the Products We Knew as Children
Mom's Frugality Lasted Longer
than the Great Depression.
August 20, 2016

My mother was frugal, religiously so. Both she and Lee's mother raised children during the Great Depression, and that likely had something to do with their economies.

I can't say what thrift measures my mother-in-law carried throughout her life, but she did frequently say, "If I had a nickel for every pound of hamburger I've cooked, I'd be a wealthy woman."

The best Depression-era story Lee told on his mother was that she wrapped the ice for the ice box in newspaper to make it last longer. Of course, insulating ice so it wouldn't melt defeated its ability to keep things cold, but I suppose, with her big family, the potential for leftover meatloaf spoiling wasn't an issue.

My mother took frugality way past the point that my friends' mothers did. I learned this when I spent the night at their houses and experienced their comforts—especially tooth paste.

My friends' families had accustomed themselves to better times after World War II, while my mom didn't yet indulge in simple luxuries. She was still picking lipstick out of the bottom of the tube with a bobby pin.

If we were out of earshot, my sister and I referred to Mom as St. Catherine, her self-denial (albeit inflicted on us all) making her eligible for beatification.

Mom bought tooth powder rather than the more desirable, more expensive toothpaste. Also, our toilet tissue was not even as soft as the cheap stuff at school. And Mom unwrapped the bar soap as soon as she brought it home from the market so it would dry out and last longer, though it was hard to work up a suds with it.

As I compared my current creature comforts to the "deprivations" of my childhood, realizations began to emerge from my subconscious.

We kids added a bit of water to the small pile of powder in the palm of our hand, and it became toothpaste. My mother didn't pay Pepsodent to add the water!

Self-indulgent me! How I'd aspired to real toothpaste! Now when I buy it, I pay for the water to be added. Lots of water, apparently. What is labeled "toothpaste" is not paste-like at all, but oozy goo that doesn't require even a squeeze or for your tooth brush to be wet, and it quickly disappears from its extra-cost, gravity-friendly, stand-up tube. Instead of where the yellow went, I wonder where real tooth paste went.

Self-indulgent me! Not only is my toilet tissue squeezable, but one option has lotion in it. Comfy but not very absorbent, it takes more sheets to serve the purpose. And—poof!—a regular roll is used up in a couple days. A "double-double roll" is about the size of the rolls we had as kids. Why is that?

Self-indulgent me! My bar soap is full of creams and vitamins and is wonderfully sudsy, but—though I unwrap bars of soap when I get them home, just like Mom did—a bar lasts only slightly longer than it takes for a banana to acquire brown spots.

So, here's the question I asked myself as I was showering the other morning: Why is my soap so sudsy, even when it's theoretically dry?

And here's the answer I came up with: It's because soap is probably infused with water—like toothpaste!

And all that softness Mr. Whipple didn't want us to squeeze? It is air, folks!

We are paying extra for virtually nothing. The inexpensive additives, which make some of today's products

180

"better" than the ones around when our mothers were in charge, are put into products for the purpose of causing them to be used up faster. We're buying more often, the manufacturers are making more money, and what we get are catchy commercials, air, and water.

We're not as attentive as our mothers, and we're surely not as frugal.

St. Catherine lived to be 100. Mother's frugal habits paid off. One of her life-long wishes was that she wouldn't be a "burden to her children," and she'd saved the money to take care of herself to the end. She didn't drink or smoke because those habits cost money. She had no heart disease, no lung disease, no cancer.

She took care of herself. She never fell for clever advertising, she stuck with Brand X soap, and she bought toilet tissue that was hard to squeeze. If she'd also exercised, she'd probably still be alive at 108.

I'd like to note that our mother would not have been considered a burden by Carolyn or me. By burden, Mom meant she didn't want to have to live with her children.

I'm glad Mom got her wish. The knowledge of our self-indulgent, squandrous ways probably would have killed her!

• • •

SIDE STORY:
This reminded me of the story about someone telling the shampoo manufacturer how he could double his sales. "How?" asked the shampoo man.

"After the instructions to lather and rinse, add the word 'Repeat,'" replied the clever fellow.

You don't fall for that, do you.

Cars are the true windows of the soul.
You Are What You Drive in Corona del Mar.
August 31, 2016

It's said that eyes are the windows of the soul, but for those not face to face, we can guess what lies within someone from what their cars tell us about them. For example, owners of cars with tinted windows are like people wearing sunglasses inside: they don't want others to look into their souls.

In the early 2000s, when Lee and I first moved to Corona del Mar, Jaguars owned the local roads. Jaguars seemed to say their owners were the classic, conservative type—and they love luxury. It's hard to distinguish the new Jaguars from other cars now or to know what they're saying.

BMWs replaced the Jaguar in local popularity. BMWs say "You don't have to be the ultimate driver to own the ultimate driving machine."

Next came all the SUVs and—for a blessedly short while—the appalling "I have no soul" Hummer. Now there's a personal statement! "I'm bigger 'n you and ready to fight!"

For a while, Bentleys replaced Hummers on the neighborhood popularity scale, saying "I have class and subtlety, and I'm richer than you and all your friends."

The Prius virtually emptied the streets of other cars. Prius drivers care about the environment and about how much they spend on gas. A Prius says "Yes, my car is funny-looking, but I can drive in the HOV lane."

The Tesla is a Bentley mated with a Prius. Tesla says, "I care about the environment, *and* I'm richer than you and all your friends."

I "shop" for my next car all the while I'm driving my present one. Some years ago, Lexus and Mercedes battled for the road, possibly because they have the nearest dealerships.

One model especially called to me, so I told the

salesman that I wanted a used C-300 with GPS.

"We might have one of those," he replied. "We can't keep them on the lot."

So I bought their lone, white C-300 with GPS. I told Jeanne—who drives her trusty old-chic BMW convertible and actually *is* the ultimate driver—"The reason they call it the C-300 is because every day, you see 300."

Of the ubiquitous model, the ubiquitous-est is white. When I got mine home, I put "lipstick" on it to distinguish it amid the horde.

That means bumper stickers.

The first was CodePink's shiny fuchsia one: this nonprofit organization demonstrates for peace and protests globally against injustice toward women.

I like luxury cars, but my bumper-stickers tend to contradict what my cars say. My C-300 said, "I'm of the conservative crowd, at the low end of the classy scale" while my bumper statements say, "I'm liberal. And tacky."

My prior conservative classic car screamed "flaming liberal" and accumulated two dozen stickers by the 2008 presidential election year.

That sounds like a lot, but not all stickers are for bumpers. Some are small window stickers, like the ones my grandkids send from their colleges. Although the Dartmouth grad already graduated with her J.D. from NYU and has her own practice, her colleges remained affixed. They don't call 'em "stickers" for nothing.

My other little stickers have included the equals sign that denotes the NAACP, the rainbow for LGBT, and my all-time fave: "If you're not outraged, you're not paying attention."

The first bumper sticker I had, on my 1959 clunker, was "No war toys." I was a bit of a liberal even when I was registered otherwise. I suspect there's some of the opposite political philosophy in all of us.

Lots of people react to my bumper stickers. One man castigated me as being blasphemous because of a sticker asserting that the Lord would never carry a gun or vote Republican.

Sometimes I get a scrawled note insulting me. But sometimes I get a nice note.

Either way, Gelson's parking lot is an arena for expressing partisanship. A woman once stopped me to say she'd felt she was the only one who thought like she did in all of Orange County

When strangers speak to me of our common political beliefs, I always hug them. One woman said, "Come to think of it, you hugged me when you had your previous car, too."

While my mind shouts "Yes!" my soul just won't say "Prius."

I traded my much-loved C-300 for something sporty and red. It says that I like things that are sporty. And red. It's not a particularly popular model. I don't always buy the most popular. I surely skipped Hummer season.

Maybe by 2020, Tesla will be selling used Model 3s. By then, the promised entry-level electric luxury car could be both debugged and compatible with my budget.

I'll buy one on Lee's behalf. He had an EV-1 in mind in the 1980s, but he never had a chance to own one.

So, honey, you'll be able to tell your WWII buddies Up There that you were one of the first to want an electric car and, at last, your wifey has one.

Even without cars in heaven, they know you are a good soul.

• • •

Single seniors website gets me thinking.
Playing the Match Game Can Be Tricky.
September 10, 2016

A while back, Terry Goldstein wrote a piece in the Pilot imagining what it would be like to attend a seniors' speed-dating event. She made it sound really funny!

But I'm sorry that, once I'd worked up the courage to sign up for the one at the local OASIS, the waiting list was full. My friend Annie had encouraged me to do it. In plenty of time.

It's been over three years since Lee died, and in addition to missing him, I've begun to miss doing the things we did together—playing bridge, attending social events and the movies. It's no fun to go places alone, and woman friends don't fill the void. (Sorry, women friends.)

I wish I could just fill out a form about what I want in a social companion and have him delivered by UPS.

My daughter Jan suggested I try a single-seniors website. She'd joined one and met a nice guy, so . . . Mom?

OK. I joined the website, but only for a month. Jan and I discovered that we got sent the same men as "matches"— despite our different ages and preferences! Bru-ther!

I've never sent so many messages and received so few replies. Pretty sure it had to do with listing myself as a liberal, but what would be the point in *not* warning potential significant others? Another negative was that I said I was looking for a bridge partner.

Of the scads of profiles I've read, conservatives outnumber liberals about 50 to one, and the only liberal who played bridge had already met his match. I felt rejected on every level—age, political philosophy, and bridge-playing.

So I bought a sporty bright red car and felt way better for a while. I love the car, but going places with it isn't the same as going with Lee. Amid its many special new features, a warm hand to hold when the light is red is not included.

So I joined what I thought was a different site. It turned out to be the same one with a different name. A "sister site." A clone, I'd say. Same faces. Same matches.

The thing that started me thinking about telling this story, though, is a question you can ask to facilitate communication with someone interested in you: "If you had to leave everything behind but five things, what would they be?"

Wow! So much stuff! I suppose we acquired it because it fills up the horizontal surfaces. OK, the tchotchkes of a lifetime are just going to have to stay behind.

And my new bamboo pillow I bought at the O.C. Fair. What would I take? Not clothes. At packing time, Lee used to say, "Don't worry about what to pack. You can always buy what you need when you get there." He was such a practical, sensible guy.

I suppose putting the five things in a vehicle is a given, because it didn't say I had to carry them. It also didn't say I was going to jail, or I'd just take books, pens and paper.

I finally decided on these items: family photos; my computer; selected books; money access for survival; and my sense of humor, such as it is. Wait. Like taking your brain or heart, sense of humor would be a given. So, OK, I'd take my hearing aids.

What would you take?

Most people's first choice would be their cell phones, I bet. A phone *could* come in handy, though. I suppose I could take my phone and leave my hearing aids. If someone faces me so I can read their lips, I hear fairly well without hearing aids.

Anyway, I really liked that question. I put my answer into my profile. (In the singles' website jargon, your profile is where you tell about yourself and about the sort of person you're seeking.)

I've been more successful in getting replies this time around, even with "liberal" in my self-description. In a message to a potential match, I ask if the person is real or just clip art. Maybe it gives them a laugh. (And maybe they're clip art.) Still, several fellows have alluded to getting together with me.

But I feel a lot of anxiety about that. Do I have to give them my phone number? I can tell my mindset is negative because my first thought was "Thank goodness I bought those call-blocking phones."

Do I really want to meet someone face-to-face? I know I'll compare everyone with Lee. Could I feel favorable toward anyone?

So, at the magical age of 77, I'm feeling alone, or greedy, or needing something more than all the wonderful things already in my life.

I'll give it another chance—but only for a month.

• • •

AFTER STORY:
Carol, my friend at my high school's alumnae office, sent me this email after she read the story.

"I laughed with your wanting to get the perfect person by filling out an order form for UPS delivery. Many a time while looking through catalogues, I have been tempted to ask for the 'gentleman on page 35 in the blue polo shirt, but I do not see his item number.'"

Food fads forever, but not kale!
Food Trends Come and Go, but Hold the Kale:
September 18, 2016

I can speak only for Southern California, and only for a small part of that. I've noticed, ever since Caesar salads, that foods suddenly appear at the same moment on restaurant menus everywhere. Caesars showed up in the '70s, I think. They're still here, and I still love 'em.

Not just in restaurants. My mother might say food fads date at least as far back as home-made salmon croquettes. What the heck was a croquette? Betcha that wouldn't trend for a second go-round.

I'd say my generation's response to salmon croquettes was Beef Stroganoff, in the 1960s. I liked making it, up to the point when I added the sour cream and the sauce curdled—yuck! Although it also uncurdled, I preferred plain buttered noodles. But, to our guests, that dish meant I'd made a fuss over them.

In my memory, chip-and-dip was from the 1950s, an at-home party dish—crinkle-cut potato chips and Lipton's dry onion soup mix added to sour cream. Served with gimlets or daiquiris.

The restaurants' answer was hot artichoke-spinach-cheese dip, with low-cal veggies to scoop up the high-cal ingredients. Available most anywhere there's a Happy Hour.

Happy Hour! When did that sprout up like flowers in springtime—bringing deep-fried, bacon-and-cheese-stuffed potato skins. So good! And so bad for us.

Cheese fondue with bread chunks was the party food of the 1960s.

Also, salad bars started popping up then. Lee was a big salad bar fan. He'd select things I never served at home in a salad—capers, raisins, sunflower seeds, and pickled beets, topped with cottage cheese. Otherwise, he was perfect.

As if a newly passed law governed them, in the '70s and '80s, pot-lucks weren't complete without 3-bean salad, Ambrosia salad (fruit, mayo, marshmallows, and coconut), and a casserole of Campbell's mushroom soup with french-cut green beans.

And about then, Mud Pie showed up on menus.

Wine and cheese parties? Everywhere as of the '70s. LOTS of wines. A dozen kinds of cheese. ("From the lips to the hips.")

Before wine, people drank cocktails, like they're supposed to. And ate the Chex Mix.

Off the subject, somewhat. Why did it become that you can't have friends over to play bridge unless you feed them a six-course dinner with three kinds of wine? My mother told me never to arrive at a party hungry so I snack-up before I leave home and return feeling gi-normous.

It's *impossible* to say "Thank you, but I'm too full for your time-consuming, home-made lemon-supreme molten-chocolate bananas-Foster delight."

I tell myself it's Jello and will only fill in the cracks. Which is why I lie about my weight on my driver's license.

In my parents' era, they invited friends to play bridge, served Planter's Spanish peanuts and a cocktail, plus dessert at the end of the evening and coffee for the road.

For an actual cocktail party, they served pigs-in-a-blanket, or, God forbid, that "potted meat product" I loved as a child: Vienna sausages. I couldn't possibly eat one now that I've read the ingredients label. Vienna sausages are meat like Velveeta is cheese or SPAM is ham.

And SPAM's back! In restaurants!!

At least Velveeta makes a good *chile con queso* dip.

Quiche and Cajun-blackened fish appeared in the early 1980s.

I made trays and trays of broiled rumaki for parties back then.

That's also when I met Cold Duck. The first time we offered it to friends, they said, "No thanks. We've just eaten." Mmm. Cold Duck. Still a fave of mine—with popcorn and cribbage. Calling "pink champagne" Cold Duck was clever marketing, similar to what made low-esteem rosé wines popular—calling them white Zinfandel or white Burgundy. "White" rosés appeared overnight on every wine list.

I actually believe wine is falling out of style. Last time I had a family party, the guests drank mostly designer beers and Margaritas. Maybe it was the balance of youth to age, or maybe it's the 2010s.

I'll have a well-vodka martini up, with a twist, please.

In the 1990s, it was goat cheese and Chinese Chicken salad.

And all the above food lead to the South Beach Diet in the 2000s. With caffeine, a là Starbucks.

Maybe ten years ago, wedge salads debuted everywhere, like the nationwide opening of a movie. I guess people had to eat a quarter of a head of iceberg lettuce with bacon and blue cheese for lunch to counteract the sweet potato fries they'd consumed yesterday.

And speaking of salad, what happened to that orange French dressing? No, not Milani's 1890—the other one. I liked that on *salade Nicoise!* Everything is balsamic now.

What instantly made sushi a national dish? And chicken-and-waffles?

Macaroni and cheese, that creamy stuff we children of Catholic mothers ate on Fridays, formerly a humble and homely dish, is now on menus everywhere—truffled, three-cheesed, and batter-fried.

And now there's the ubiquitous pork belly. Don't tell me it's bacon! If pork bellies are bacon, call them bacon!! Being bacon is dandy *as is!*

I remember when "pork bellies" was only a commodity, part of the morning market report on the family Philco.

For a while, the newbie food was quinoa (pronounced keen-wah) as a salad additive. Now it's kale.

Kale. Really? Will this menu option last as long as Caesar salad and Mud Pie?

Kale. Yuck!

Quick! Refresh my palate with salted caramel sorbet!

• • •

The Resurgence of Home Cookin'
Eating Restaurant-style at Home
October 15, 2016

I used to love to cook. Now I panic at the thought of putting an actual meal together. Having guests is beyond my capacity—an economic boon for the local restaurants. And everybody gets what they like.

It's not that I love to eat out, but every restaurant meal yields leftovers for two meals I don't have to prepare.

I have a big collection of freezer-perfect take-home containers.

I love my microwave.

I had dived into cooking for my blended family. I'd already found the way to Lee's heart, and I quickly learned that the way to his kids' hearts was to feed them a variety of good meals. Dinners averaged nine of us in the first year.

Everyone's favorite dinner was flank steak with mushroom gravy, rice, and Green Giant Broccoli with Cheese Sauce. And black olives for Lee. But to keep them coming back, I didn't do that more than every couple weeks.

Thanksgiving dinner was my Personal Best. The family would be ready for seconds before I sat down for firsts. (I had to do some retraining there.)

I thought nothing of cooking for a large group of friends. I had a cooking-for-50 cookbook.

Oh, where is that girl of yesteryear, the one who could do anything? Her older self cooks only whatever all goes in one pot—soups, stews, lamb shanks. Costco's cooked lamb shanks are as good as the ones I could simmer for three hours.

The decades passed, along with my motivation for combining ingredients. I even hate to go the market—though not because

192

of the bumper-sticker critics.

My friend Brian recommended "HomeCookin'" [pseudonym]—fresh ingredients for meals, delivered to your doorstep.

You choose from delectable options on the website's menu, and the following week, you receive everything you need. Except salt, pepper, and olive oil.

The first carton arrived as promised—two meals for two people twice. That's eight meals for me, at a fraction of restaurant prices.

I could barely lift the box. The ice-substitute alone weighed 20 pounds.

In the kitchen, I unpacked and froze the meat entree that I wouldn't be using yet. The veggie packages—clearly labeled and containing their unique ingredients—I refrigerated.

Also came the recipes. The first meal would be Asian meatballs with ponzu sauce, snap peas, and rice. OK, so some assembly is required. Nothing is perfect.

I sliced and diced. I blended the ground pork with fresh green onion, garlic and ginger, and the pre-measured packets of spices and flour. I poured sesame oil from a tiny bottle into the skillet.

While the rice cooked, I browned and frowned. The meatballs wouldn't stay round.

OK, a stir-fry would do, a là ponzu.

Lesson one: I can use the ingredients however I want!

Truly, dinner was restaurant-level delicious.

I divided the remainder into one small and one large El Ranchito container, freezing the big one.

Generally I run the dishwasher only every five days. I know, because I count the cocktail glasses. But each pot, pan, cutting board and utensil needed to be degreased. I filled the empty dishwasher to capacity.

Lesson two: Choose recipes requiring less paraphernalia.

The next week another weighty carton arrived, the ingredients including two giant ears of corn, two yams and an onion.

I emptied the ice packets into my soup kettle, as I had before, the eight solid slabs nearly filling it, once defrosted. The plastic packaging is recyclable, and the melted ice-type-stuff can be disposed of like water, though not by drinking. Nor by watering plants either, as it leaves a glutinous residue.

Artificial ice, defrosted, is the consistency of . . . Sorry, I have no frame of reference for this substance. Just, it works OK for running the garbage disposal, with some extra water to rinse down the gunky remains.

Lesson three: If you "grill" a steak and corn on the cob in a regular skillet, it can take three days of soaking and scraping to clean the skillet. [Message to self: Buy non-stick skillet.]

For the fourth meal, I set about making pork loin with fig sauce.

I brought out the ingredients and read the instructions, realizing that I hadn't defrosted the pork. No problem. By floating it in a dishpan of cold water, it would be ready to cook by the time I finished my martini and a few rounds of Canasta on the computer.

I roasted my prepped carrots and Brussels sprouts while I seared the meat, smoking up the kitchen. Before the alarm could go off, I turned on the range-fan, making it impossible to hear my recording of "Jeopardy."

I was supposed to sear the meat on three sides, but this meat screamed to be seared on four sides. I spent the extra time drinking the two ounces of wine I had put out that was supposed to attract a sudden home-invasion of fruit flies, but didn't.

As the veggies finished roasting along with the pork roast, I emptied the container of red wine and the pot of fig jelly into the searing pan and stirred it into a fragrant sauce.

The next step was to "plate the dish." How cute is that phrase! I considered photographing the results, but it seemed just too self-congratulatory.

Eating at home can be creative, delicious, and delightful! I suppose I could even have occasional guests over for Liz's "HomeCookin'."

Oh!

Lesson four: Those fruit flies? They can't resist defrosted artificial ice!

• • •

AFTER STORY:
Readers didn't believe that the fruit flies actually went for the slushy artificial ice, but they really, truly did.

But if I were a fruit fly about to dive to my death, I'd go for the wine.

26.2 Miles Across the Sea on the Catalina Flyer
Catalina Island Is Still Waiting for Me.
November 19, 2016

I've visited Catalina Island maybe a dozen times, once staying overnight with my parents when I was about ten. After we moved here from Kansas in 1945, my mom made sure our family saw all the wondrous attractions of the Greater Los Angeles area.

Though I grew up near Wilshire and LaBrea, we'd first lived for a while at B102 in Surfside, so when I say we saw everything from the orange groves to the Planetarium and from Olvera Street to Ocean Park, you'd get the idea. Such fond memories . . .

In turn, I introduced our big family to our "big neighborhood," including vacationing with all of us and our in-laws on Balboa Island—which is when I decided I wanted to live down here.

When I got the urge to take my girls on a get-away this year, I first considered Hawaii, but Britt (my "daughter-in-love") wasn't able to handle the four long flights from JFK and back.

So we locals decided to fly to New York, and we could all cruise to Canada. We could tour Manhattan! See shows! Shop on 5th Avenue! And on the way home, we could visit granddaughter Sally in Charleston!

The more elaborate the plans got, the less enthusiasm my local daughters had for the trip. Cheryl would have to board her menagerie longer, and Jan would miss work, and, and, and. Eventually, Britt felt up to traveling here.

But what fun is it to vacation where we've all lived?

My computer-guru friend Brian suggested Catalina.

"I've never been to Catalina!" said Jan.

"You've never been to Catalina?" I'd slipped up on that.

"I haven't been to Catalina in years!" said Cheryl.

"Anything's fine with me," said Britt.

Brian assured me there was enough to do on Catalina to keep us busy for days, and the game was afoot.

Lee and I had connected with our travel agent Renee [REE-nee] 30 years ago when she helped us plan our first cruise. Since then she's secured flights and accommodations for the whole family. Renee's planned more trips that I've had to cancel than most travel agents plan for most families in a lifetime. (Recent examples: Hawaii and Canada.)

When I presented her with the challenge of finding a place for the four of us on Catalina, she was up for it.

"The girls all need their own rooms," I told her. "Is that do-able?"

"It's post-season," Renee said. "Let me check out a few things and get back to you." (I wonder how many times she's told me that over the years. I could hear her voice as I typed this.)

My favorite option was a four-bedroom apartment in Grisham House, directly across the bay from the Casino and steps from the sand (what little of it there is).

Our downstairs neighbors were a jet-ski rental, a t-shirts shop, and a psychic. We got excited about the psychic, but she'd taken her crystal ball and gone home for the winter.

I'd packed books, a cribbage board, playing cards, rummy cubes, a jigsaw puzzle, and coloring books, colored pencils, brush markers, and felt-tips.

My luggage weighed a ton and all I'd brought to wear were two extra sweatshirts and another pair of jeans. Oh! And four matching sweatshirts I'd had made for us, which said "Catalina Island 2016" beneath a row of seashells.

We loved our apartment! But we barely more than slept and showered there. We were exhausted at the end of each jam-packed day and just chatted and colored as we recovered from the fun activities between breakfast and dinner.

We shopped galore. I didn't recall so many delightful shops! When my parents took me, Catalina was known for straw hats and hula skirts, the salt water taffy puller, and t-shirts, but the souvenirs we found on this trip were beautiful and unique.

Wind chimes for Britt. A decorative tile picture for Jan. A suede fringed purse for Cheryl (like one she'd had in the '70s). Art glass for me. Oh, and for some lucky others, a toy stuffed squid, a velvet witch's hat, and a Cubs' baseball cap.

Avalon was a-wave with Cubs flags during the World Series because Wrigley's teams trained there.

Speaking of Wrigley, we went to the mansion for lunch and a tour. It's extraordinary, and the view of the harbor is glorious.

We also went on a complete tour of the Casino, which, if you don't already know, was *never* a gambling casino, and a night-time ghost tour.

The best tour was the "Taste of Catalina"—tastings at six different restaurants, alternating savories and sweets, paired with alcoholic beverages for those who imbibe.

Or maybe my favorite thing was renting the golf cart and the four of us toodling all over the island and laughing for three hours.

No. The best thing was everything—making memories with my daughters that might someday turn out to be adventures for them and *their* daughters.

• • •

Comparing Books to Movies and Vice Versa
The Movie Can Improve the Book (or Not).
November 27, 2016

I've been a reader since we kids voluntarily went to the library to get books to read during the summer. You couldn't just roller skate, play in the creek, ride bikes, and play hide-and-seek and tag and Cootie for three months!

I've also been a movie-lover since I was a child. My family went to the movies when it was convenient for our parents, seldom at the time the movie began. This gave rise to my father's famous saying—used when we kids rambled on—"This is where I came in."

When we moved to Los Angeles after World War II, my mother took me to premieres. To me, the pink searchlights were as enchanting as the fur-clad actresses. I think the searchlights were left over from WWII. For a long time after, grand openings used them to attract customers.

Jeanne, Sharon, Mary Ellyn, and I went to free movies on Saturdays. I must have seen "Heidi" a half dozen times. (In my mind's ear, I can hear Shirley Temple shouting "Grandfather! Grandfather!") The theaters showed cartoons, a cliff-hanger, and an old feature film—if not "Heidi," then "National Velvet" or a Hopalong Cassidy movie. Once, it was "Frankenstein." There were no GP or R ratings then. If the Legion of Decency didn't object, it was fine with our folks. FYI, parents: "Frankenstein" gives little kids nightmares.

For many years, I liked reading a book if a movie was to be made of it.

The book "Rosemary's Baby" (1967) scared me so much I had to say the Rosary before I could fall asleep. I hadn't been so frightened since I'd seen "Frankenstein," and I hadn't said the Rosary since the 1950s.

Of course, that didn't stop me from seeing the film. I

took Jan, my daughter-to-be, with me. She'd read the book, too. The movie was just as good, but because we knew the outcome, the scare factor was pretty much eliminated.

Sometimes books are better than movies, and sometimes vice versa. Sometimes I'd read a book and wouldn't want to see the movie, like "The Exorcist."

Some people who'd read "Snow Falling on Cedars" didn't want to see the movie because they were afraid it might ruin the book. But I thought the book made the movie better, and the movie made the book better.

Being a writer, if I've read the book, I tend to consider whether the movie is true to the author's intent. Imagine trying to cram a story that fills 400 pages into a two-hour film!

My most heart-swelling movie experience was seeing J. K. Rowling's fantastical visions actualized in "Harry Potter and the Sorcerer's Stone." I cried. Not at the cruelty of Harry's step-family nor the joy of his rescue by Hagrid. I cried because I SAW staircases move. Because I SAW Quidditch being played. Because the author's words were given life, perfectly.

I read "Miss Peregrine's Home for Peculiar Children" and then saw the movie, and I liked the book better. Seemed to me the movie made unnecessary changes and cuts and added much that wasn't in the book. So boo on the producers of that one!

I read "The Girl on the Train" before seeing the movie. I'd expected it would be like reading "Gone Girl" and then seeing that—clearer as to the settings, keeping the most important parts of the story, both book and movie satisfying.

But no! It's thumbs down from me! "Girl on the Train" was all close-ups of a distressed woman whose hand shook too much to put on lipstick but apparently could apply mascara to smudge beneath her widened eyes in every scene. (That's just my favorite complaint, not my only one.) My friend June had warned me, and my friend Eileen said she'd walked out.

So I wondered whether it worked better to see the movie, and if I liked it, then read the book.

I loved seeing "The Dressmaker" and went directly to Barnes & Noble to purchase the book. Ugh. The way-better movie started in the middle of the action. I'd read a third of the book before dressmaking was even mentioned. And I don't like what the book did to her only friend in town either.

I'll probably skip buying a book after I've enjoyed a movie.

I almost always finish a book I've started, but I've walked out of three movies. I don't know if they were books—"Brubaker" (brutal, but nominated for Best Screenplay); "The Unforgiven" (brutal, but won Best Picture); and "Cocktail" (brutal because Tom Cruise was, like, drunk on himself, and rated 5% on Rotten Tomatoes).

I wonder why they don't have premieres with searchlights anymore. Maybe because of the over-exposure of celebrities on television and computers.

I miss the searchlights.

• • •

A Traditional Christmas Shopping Excursion
This Friendship Certainly Is a Holiday Gift.
December 17, 2016

Jeanne and I made a date for our traditional trip to the Junior League's Christmas Company.

My horoscope that day said my relationship with someone who makes me laugh is a "slice of heaven." Jeanne's said she might feel like she's being forced to have fun, but pretending could turn into reality.

I told her about our horoscopes as we were leaving our community. She said she didn't believe in that stuff, and I said I hoped she could pretend.

Under the Fairgrounds archway, I realized I'd left our tickets on my desk. Jeanne, who is smarter than I am by 150 percent, said they could pull up the tickets on my phone.

"No," I said. "Really?"

"Pretty sure," she said. "Something similar happened to me once."

To Jeanne? Really?

A quick-thumbed young woman worked magic on my phone, found the email with the tickets, and waved us toward the entrance, all in ten seconds.

Once inside, Jeanne and I should have had shopping carts! What a selection of virtually irresistible items!

I bought a baby gift at the first nook and picked out some gifts for my grand-family at the second, and gift tags with check boxes, like: "I hope you [check one]: enjoy; enjoy re-gifting; enjoy returning this gift."

They also had giant pick-up sticks! "Look! Just like when we were kids! Only bigger, for our older eyes." Jeanne pulled me away before I bought the giant pick-up sticks, too. She always beat me at that game anyway. And jacks.

I asked the women to put all the charges on my card.

Jeanne said, no, she would pay for her own gift tags. I said, "You paid for the parking." She said, "You paid for my ticket." I said she could buy me a glass of wine. She said, "No! I'll pay for my own purchases!"

One of the lovely proprietors said, "You guys have been friends for a long time, huh."

I said, "Jeanne has been bossing me around for seventy years."

"Yes," Jeanne said. "And she still needs to be told more than once."

That cracked me up. It also cracked up the women. And Jeanne.

And—unbelievable!—at the next booth was a charm bracelet with pictures from the old Nancy Drew books! "Oh, buy it, Nancy J!" I said. "Don't you want it, Nancy L?" she said. "You buy it! I'll buy this pendant—the silhouette of Nancy with her magnifying glass." "You're sure you don't want the bracelet?"

It went like that, Jeanne and I bantering about our "finds."

On our way out, we noticed some gorgeous handmade, hand-beaded evening bags. Surely there was someone on my gift list who needed a hand-beaded bag! Shaleel told us he made the bags himself and his mother did the bead work. Wow.

Jeanne gave me her opinion of which were best and who should get what and wandered off. How mean! Did she expect me to make the final decision by myself? I could give two of them as gifts. Or maybe three. Shaleel gave me a really good bargain.

When I caught up with her, Jeanne was sitting down massaging her back on a vibrating pillow. "There's a bargain on them if we buy two," she said. "I don't think I need one," I said. [As I type this, I wish I'd bought the vibrating pillow.]

Jeanne asked about the purses. I told her I'd bought five because I couldn't decide which three to buy. Jeanne liked them all—so long as one in particular went to the person she felt would like it best. So I forgave her, though she hadn't known I'd thought she'd been mean to desert me.

We stopped at Filomena's on the way home, and I ordered the house Chianti while Jeanne studied the wine list.

"See, I don't cultivate taste in wines for the same reason that I don't have pierced ears."

"Stop right there," she said, laughing. "It sounds like it should be your next story for the Pilot. Don't spoil it for me."

"But . . . "

"OK, you can tell me, and then I can say, 'I know. She told me.'"

I laughed. "It's because there are too darn many earring choices I'd have to make every day," I said. "Look at how long it takes you to pick out a wine—and how long it took me to pick out a hand-beaded bag."

"Five hand-beaded bags."

"Exactly."

Happy holidays! May your horoscopes bring you much laughter with dear old friends.

• • •

Memories Wrapped in Tissue Paper
Cold Weather Has Me Contemplating Fur, Gloves.
December 29, 2016

I was thrilled to be invited to the home of dear friends in Boulder, Colorado, for Thanksgiving. Jen and Mo live almost against the Flatirons of the Rockies.

I was afraid of freezing to death. The first things into my suitcase were bed socks.

I am a thin-blooded Southern California girl. How would I keep warm as we shopped on Black Friday and Small-Stores Saturday? It could be as cold as 40 degrees!

Lee always said I have a one-degree comfort range of 72, but I'm actually good down to 68 with a sweatshirt.

Jen said it would be fine for me to bring an array of sweatshirts from dressy to casual, and if I needed to, I could wear my white fox fur coat when we went shopping. (It had followed me home in the early 1980s, and Lee let me keep it.)

The coat hadn't been groomed or refrigerated or even seen the light of day since animal activists made us aware that wearing animal furs was inhumane.

But I couldn't have given it away. If it was shameful for me to wear it, no one should wear it.

But surely in snow country it would be acceptable.

So I took it out of its mesh bag, vacuumed it, hung it outdoors, and Febrezed it.

My local friends gave me advice: Wear boots! Take scarves! Don't forget gloves!

I practiced wearing my boots for a day to determine if I would be able to wear them for three days. I haven't worn 2-inch heels since I opted for my comfort-clothes wardrobe.

Ouch! No boots then. Socks and loafers or socks and dressy flats would have to do.

Scarves? I have dozens in my drawer. They attract me

to buy them, but they don't attract me to wear them.

Although . . . I do have a pink chenille scarf and matching gloves that I wore in January 2007 when Lee and I marched down the Mall and around the Capitol, demonstrating with CodePink in Washington, DC.

Into the suitcase with those! But I couldn't wear them with my fur coat.

My reversible all-weather jacket went into the suitcase.

Gloves? In my youth, a lady was never seen without them! Nobody wears them anymore. I think it was in the '60s that women stopped wearing gloves to church and out to dinner.

I'd wrapped my mother's gloves in tissue paper after she died, and I'd wrapped my own accumulation with them.

Mom's collection includes several pair of white cotton and white kid gloves, lovely rose-colored gloves, and black gloves, including one pair with small gold studs above the wrist.

I unwrapped my own gloves, too. Small white gloves from my grammar school years. String gloves, probably for church at Eastertide. White full-length prom gloves, ruched along the seams, from my high school years. Black mid-length gloves I wore with my late-'50s college-years' smashing black cashmere coat with the push-up bat sleeves, and a chiffon scarf over my head—like Audrey Hepburn wore hers—with the ends wrapped around and tied at the back of my neck.

Early in my divorce years, my mother gave me red leather driving gloves, after I'd bought my very first car, to wear when I drove to work in the cold San Fernando Valley mornings. Seeing those red gloves again brought tears to my eyes.

My last pair of gloves are perforated leather, camel-colored riding gloves, bought when I was horseback riding in the 1990s. Riding is the best workout in the world for your stomach muscles. I was at my most trim and fit then, before the horse threw me and I decided I'd had enough of that kind of fun (and fitness).

So my last pair of gloves went back into tissue paper, back into the corner of my scarves-drawer for my California great-granddaughters to reminisce over one day. ("What are these?" they'll wonder. "Could they be, like, bed socks for your hands?")

I tucked my mother's black gloves with the studs into the pockets of my fur coat.

We had a glorious time! The daytime temperatures in Boulder were in the low-60s. I was warm enough to be comfortable in my sweatshirt and all-weather jacket as we shopped in the charming stores. I never even needed the gloves.

I wore my white fox only in the airports. No one looked at me accusingly, and it even got a lot of compliments.

• • •

Self-driving Vacuum Technology
Don't Want a Pet? How about a Robotic Vacuum?
January 12, 2017

For Christmas I bought myself the sort of gift you don't want to receive from your spouse. A vacuum cleaner.

After Lee died, friends and family suggested I get a cat or a dog. Not having grown up with pets, I didn't think befriending one would be fair to the pet. I'm known for neglecting house-plants. I have alt-plants.

A single friend asked, "No pets? What do you have to come *home* to? What reason do you have to get *up* in the morning?"

What? I come home to my *stuff*. I get up to enjoy *life*.

To stop the "Get a pet" lobby, I joked, "I'll buy one of those robot vacuum cleaners if I'm lonely.

"Honey, I'm home," I'll say," and at the sound of my voice, it will greet me at the door."

This year I truly began to feel the void. Not the one in my heart, but the one in my home, in my life.

So, I ordered the robotic vacuum. When it was delivered, I opened the box and slapped it back shut. Parts!? It had lots of *parts*.

I asked my former co-author and good friend Bill if he'd put it together for me.

He indicated he was put-together-ly challenged, but if it came with an instruction manual, he could probably do it.

While he was deep in the quarter-inch-thick manual, I began to unload the box.

The big round robot itself. The charging base and an electrical connection for it. Two replacement filters. Three screws and a screwdriver. An extra revolving brush. A comb. Two 4-pointed walrus mustaches. Six rubber bumpers the size and shape of emery boards. And a flying-saucer-looking thingy.

I looked at the quick-start card and figured out that just one of the whiskered attachments was necessary, requiring one of the enclosed screws.

When I began screwing it in, Bill said, "Liz, I thought you wanted me to do it."

Well, of course I did when I *asked* him, but it had begun to look like fun.

Instead of elbowing into the project, I put our lunch dishes into the dishwasher while Bill continued reading the manual.

"It looks like that whisk does go where you were trying to put it," Bill said.

I decided I was back on the team and plugged the cord into the charging station and the charger into the wall beneath the extra kitchen chair. "It needs ten clear feet in front of it, the quick-start card says. Do you think that's ten feet?"

"Yes, about that," Bill said, looking up from the manual.

When we introduced the two metal plates of the robot onto the two sticky-outy things on the charging base, the robot lit up like the news ticker in Times Square, colored lights flickering and dashes racing across the display.

I began to examine the flying-saucer.

"It's a remote control!" I said. "I thought these things got programmed and ran themselves."

"Batteries not included," Bill said.

"Ha-HAH! Have I got batteries. All sizes of batteries!" I went to the refrigerator and pulled out two double-A's.

"It takes triple-A's." Bill said.

"Well, rats. I can't find the triple-A's. I just bought some for the gizmo that adjusts my bed."

Bummer! We couldn't try out the robot.

After Bill loosened the top of my soap dispenser and loaded four bags of closet rejects into my car for delivery to the Assistance League, he was ready to head home.

Thanks, Bill!

Soon I remembered I'd put the triple-A batteries next to my bed, where I'd need them. I inserted two into the remote control and pushed Go.

The robot sounded like a leaf blower.

Not quite ten feet later, it ran into a chair and by trial and error it proceeded to explore my kitchen. It was like watching your bathroom scale play blind-man's-buff. Every time it bumped into something, it made a 30-degree turn. There appears to be no in-built patterning that tells it where it's been or where it hasn't.

I laughed so hard I snorted. I'm surprised no one has posted a video on Facebook or YouTube.

I named it 'Putchie-tookums,' and I need to put those bumper strips on him.

Bill called, asking how the robot worked.

"Well, so far it needs to be told when to turn right and left, but it does pick up stuff in its path. I didn't find a way to program it. Maybe once it knows its way around, it'll program itself."

"Well, I'm glad it's working," he said. "We're a good team."

"Always have been," I said.

I don't expect to be able to get the little robot to meet me at the door with a martini, but I can envision returning home and calling out, "Putchie-tookums, I'm home!"

And . . . *vroooom.*

• • •

Looking for a Cargo Purse
Speak Softly, but Carry a Big Purse.
February 3, 2017

Lee and I used to travel a lot, and I found a perfect travel purse with pockets for absolutely everything, even a slot for a collapsible fan for the tropics. Places for pens, eyeglasses, camera, phone (as if I use my phone), passport, maps, a Michelin guide, meds, wallet, makeup, snack, address book, novel, curling iron (just kidding about the curling iron)—anything you could possibly want to carry with you for a day of sightseeing.

For travel by plane, I put my big purse and book and documents into a giganto Vera Bradley diaper bag, which REALLY has a lot of pockets!

The thing is . . . I want to carry almost everything with me when I'm *not* traveling. Except possibly the Michelin and the fan.

I am a little person who is a big-purse person.

So I carry my old washable travel purse—with the slash-guard shoulder strap and zipper lock—all the time. Or, I did. It began to show signs of wear, with the white cord showing through the black piping. A permanent marker can only do so much to hide that.

I so admire women who change bags when they change outfits.

I looked through my collection of purses the other day, thinking it's time for me to show some class (if it didn't shrivel from neglect after I transitioned to my comfort-clothes wardrobe),

I have a lovely brown-and-black weave Brighton bag, virtually new, though I bought it years ago. I have some black purses—even an elegant, thin, lady-like purse. I also have a shabby-chic brown bag that looks like you could put a buffalo in it. Disappointing. Not one of them has enough pockets.

You could say purses "grew" on me.

Remember when all you needed to carry were your Esterbrook pen, a comb, a Chapstick, and a dime to call home? In the early 1950s, felt "envelope" purses accommodated those things. Small and flat, they came in a zillion colors.

Remember basket purses? You put in your comb, lipstick, ballpoint pen, little address book, and wallet with all your friends' pictures in it, and tied a small scarf around one edge of the handle for whimsey. In our peasant blouses and our skirts with a dozen petticoats, we looked like we were headed for the picnic in the musical "Oklahoma!"

Do you remember big vinyl, draw-string shoulder bags? There was almost enough room for my school notebook in mine. If my ballpoint pen leaked, I'd could scrub the ink off with cleanser. I suppose today's equivalent would be a washable backpack.

Last time I went shopping with granddaughter Sally—a little person who is not a big-purse person—she was looking for a big purse. Sally, a lawyer in Charleston, wanted a shoulder bag with enough room for her laptop and her legal files. On the East Coast, I gathered, such bags were common goods then, but in SoCal, not so much.

Do you remember when men carried purses? I'd wondered how they'd gotten along without them for all the years!

And now, no "male bags." Men put their cell phones in their shirt or front pants pockets (risking the effects of radiation) and their comb and wallet in the back pockets. Or they wear those dowdy (although functional) cargo pants.

Hmm. What I need is a *cargo purse!*

I tried a cargo jacket like the one my friend Annie uses instead of a purse. Mine had 25 pockets, and when I filled them with the contents of my purse, I felt like a pack mule. (Returned it.)

Then I followed a Groupon option and ordered a red purse with all sorts of hiding places. How could I not have a red purse?! Red is my color!

It has three sections, two with magnetic closures and one with a zipper for the stuff you don't want anyone to steal. That section has plenty of pockets. But . . .

Although it looked really perky in the photos, in person it looks like it needs to be starched and ironed. The two outside sections with magnetic closures flop open, and the zipper goes three quarters of the way around the middle and is tricky to zip against the slouchy sides. (Returned it.)

So here's the lesson. Your online Groupon might be a really good deal, but you could get a red purse with lots of pockets that simply breaks your heart.

My trusty travel purse isn't available in black anymore, but maybe it comes in red . . .

. . .

SIDE STORY:
This story was published on my sister's birthday.

My sister Carolyn was a poet and something of a gypsy. Ethereal, even. We, in the family, used to say Carolyn was *in* this world, but she wasn't *of* it.

She didn't give a fig about what anyone thought of her, and her tastes ran toward the unconventional.

For her purse, she put a medium-size office-type waste basket into a reusable grocery bag and somehow attached a roller skate or skate board—something with wheels—to the bottom. She just held onto the handles of the bag, and the purse "heeled" as if on a leash.

Darn clever, my sister. I sure do miss her.

Reflections on Christmas Presents, Past and Future
It Is Getting Pretty Late
to Put Away Holiday Spangle.
February 18, 2017

Well, here it is February and I already have all the Christmas decorations put back into the garage. Now for someone who is not afraid of climbing ladders to put them on the storage shelf.

How many of you still have Christmas presents that you bought "just in case"?

I have a half-carton of wine meant as hostess gifts (clearly, I am not on enough guest lists). A gift basket of the ingredients for Moscow Mules. Six double-decks of playing cards—because I can't resist buying them and then can't part with them. A DVD collection of old movies; a DVD collection of Shakespeare plays; and a videotape collection of movie musicals (that one's gathered the figurative dust of many Christmases). Plus assorted Christmas music CDs, designer coloring books, and other one-size-fits-nobody gifts.

It's the same with greeting cards. I buy them when I see them, and then when it's someone's birthday, anniversary, get-well time, whatever, none of the selections suits the next-up recipient.

But you can't always find a card that says what you want when you need it, and three stores later you just buy anything so you can go home.

Except for my nieces. I have six nieces I buy cards for, and believe me, you have to buy niece cards when you see them. Same with grandkids and great-grands. But when my collection of those run out . . .

Our family has grown beyond umpteen to ump-30 dearies, and with my sister's family (all mine now), there are 50 of us. A bunch of my event-greetings were late and/or ill-suited last year.

And my check register shows so many outstanding checks that my grandkids didn't deposit . . . do they not need the money, or did they tear up the checks out of the goodness of their hearts?

In November, I told the immediate family that I wasn't sending any more cards or checks, not even at Christmas.

I got only two responses to that email, and they were on the order of "What took you so long?"

I had believed that offspring think grandmothers have nothing more important to do than shower them with love they can cash, but the outstanding checks in my account made me realize that in the overall scheme, the individual amounts I gave were not life-changing.

Instead of many small checks, I could send fewer but significant checks to my fave rescue missions, where a chunk of money would do great good.

But I began to feel Grinchy. (What were the family members who didn't email me back thinking?) So I bought Christmas gifts for my family, starting with those five lovely hand-beaded bags for some of my granddaughters. I bought delightful Liberty jigsaw puzzles for families, true collectors' items—wooden puzzles that feature little figures among the pieces. I bought useful robotic vacuums for my single kids. And other stuff.

Family members of all ages really loved those puzzles. They went over bigger than the checks I'd been sending for all these years. In fact, everybody liked their presents!

Here's my "take-away"—the lessons I learned. Gifts selected for specific people, like greeting cards selected for specific people, meant more to the recipients than the checks did. And it's way more fun for me to select gifts!

I even got lovely thank-you notes from the charities, reminding me that the contributions are tax deductible (as checks to my kids and grandkids were not).

I think I'll bundle up most of those "all-purpose" gifts and contribute them to the Assistance League Thrift Shop.

Not the wine, of course.

Nor the playing cards. (For bridge . . . just in case).

• • •

Palm Trees and Sweatshirts
The Sun Soothes the Soul but Harms the Skin.
Easter Sunday, April 16, 2017

It amazes me that, despite available knowledge about skin cancer, people still get sunburned. And especially despite warnings that most sunscreens don't meet their promised SPFs.

So what if I was the only person on Waikiki wearing a sweatshirt and white jeans? I got to do what I wanted, which was to sit in the shade of a palm tree, sipping an occasional umbrella drink and reading. Having hours on end to read is a luxury for me, and doing it with the aquamarine ocean in front of me and Diamond Head to my left . . . no wonder they call Hawaii "paradise."

I know it's not everyone's vision of paradise. For instance, when my mother, in her seventies, came back from her (only) trip to Hawaii, I asked if she'd had a good time.

"They put teriyaki sauce on . . . everything," she said.

My mother wanted to travel, but my father did not. She went with a seniors group to Hawaii and also to Europe.

"How'd you like Europe?" I asked.

"It was old and dirty," she said.

I'm ecstatic that Lee and I started traveling before Mother did or I might have stayed home.

Lee and I traveled almost everywhere. It was such a privilege and, for us, a pleasure. Well, it was a pleasure once we figured out why—although we almost never argued—we fought when we traveled. Eventually I identified that it was because we had different expectations when we left home.

Lee looked forward to a vacation—getting away from work and phones, relaxing.

I looked forward to a trip—going and seeing and doing, and rush, rush, rush to cram in everything.

Cruising was the perfect compromise. Lee would go on excursions with me, and the rest of the time, he could relax, while I could take a class on how to play the ukulele (or whatever).

For me, relaxing has been a foreign concept. I suppose it's my "guilt-unless-multi-tasking" personality—or upbringing. Lee could mono-task. (Focusing solely on one thing, he was hard to distract. Getting his attention was not always easy.)

We visited Hawaii frequently. Once we'd finished sight-seeing, I became able to relax there. While Lee did crossword puzzles in the palm shade, I could read by his side.

I don't travel as much now, but I had a craving to go to Hawaii to get away from being myself. Daughters Jan and Cheryl didn't want to go to Hawaii. BFF Marian didn't want to go. But Maura, my friend who is younger by 20+ years, was eager to go.

She was a perfect travel companion! Neither of us felt like sight-seeing. We spent six days on Waikiki, laughing and chatting, eating or shopping, and—except for attending a luau and visiting a friend at Uncle Bo's—just relaxing.

Maura, a water-baby, wanted to spend time in the ocean, and that's what she did. I, covered from chin to toes, enjoyed the ocean air reading and watching people sunburn.

I haven't worn a bathing suit since I was in my late thirties. I quit sunbathing cold turkey when I learned about the hole in the ozone layer, the dangers of sun exposure, and the particular susceptibility for the fair-haired/blue-eyed of Eastern European descent. The clincher was the high risk for those who had experienced frequent sunburns in their youth.

218

I had been a "beach bunny." Each summer, the one to get the first sunburn won. Although I was of the baby-oil-and-Mercurochrome generation, I needed no help. I just won.

"Don't touch me. I'm sunburned!"—that was bragging!

Remember peeling off strips of skin that had blistered and dried? And once we'd tanned, remember how lovely pastel summer dresses looked against our tans? Ah, youth!

And to show for that carefree era, I have a heap o' brown spots. Yet, for wising-up forty years ago, I have no skin cancer. Ah, maturity!

And that takes me back to Waikiki, and to my friend Maura, who has beautiful Irish skin. Who slathered on a top-rated sunscreen regularly. Who enjoyed the beautiful Pacific "like a porpoise." Who got one heck of a sunburn.

• • •

AFTER STORY:

Lovely Maura asked me to make it clear that getting sunburned isn't her "thing." The antibiotic she was taking for an infection made her unexpectedly vulnerable to the sun's rays.

So if you're on a med that says "Keep out of the sun," that means YOU, not the pill bottle.

AFTER AFTER STORY:

During my last (I hope) read-through, I learned on the news that suntan lotion has an expiration date. Who knew?

So, you *can't* use it once each summer and hope for it to work until the container is empty!

Check the date on the bottom of your squirt bottle!

About Those Papers That Come with the Utility Bills
Utility Bills Come with Too Much Ephemera.
May 1, 2017

I have a confession. In all the years that I have been paying bills—let's say 57—I have never read any of the flyers, leaflets, pamphlets, or ads that come in the envelopes with the statements. But, having some spare time, I decided to skim a month's worth, an exercise that confirmed what I already believed.

I do not want Direct TV. I do not want to bundle anything more than is already bundled—not insurance, not cable, Internet and/or phone. I do not want a different security system.

I know that I can't argue with a utility company if their prices are about to go up or if they intend to install an Excess Flow Valve.

I know it will not affect my life if I miss out on a free movie from Cox Cable.

I know I should conserve water and electricity (and I do).

I know I should use my appliances early or late in the day (and I mostly do).

I know that if I smell gas, I shouldn't light a match. I am grateful that the Gas Company complies with proposition 65, whatever that is, for the good of my health. Yet if I hadn't known, I wouldn't have wondered.

I know that when I want a new cell phone, I will get one—without a reminder from AT&T. And I don't want to stream Taylor Swift.

I don't know why the Auto Club is hyping Papa John's Pizza and offering me multiple discounts I would never use.

I don't need a thank-you note from the Newport Beach Fire Department for my annual membership in Fire Medics.

And, again, I don't want Direct TV, no matter who

220

thinks I might or how "attractive" the offer is.

I know that if any of the services I use change policy, they don't expect me to object. Or if there's to be a public hearing, they don't expect me to attend. And if things are changing, I can't continue to receive the service if I don't accept the changes.

I know that I don't care what the inserts with my bills have to say. If it were really important, it would be on the news and my friends would be talking about it.

I also know that the Gas Company, the water and power providers, the cable and Internet and phone companies, the cell phone carrier, ADT, etc., etc.—they know I don't read that stuff! So why do they waste all that paper?

For a writer who edits several printed drafts of each new book, I probably have my nerve complaining about paper being wasted (and about the time required to read everyone else's written words), but . . .

As my role model and mentor Carolyn See (author Lisa's mother) once wrote, "Contribute to the Sierra Club, and do not feel guilty."

I bet that those insert-senders neither contribute to the Sierra Club *nor* feel guilty.

• • •

Doing it All, Just Not All at Once
There's Plenty of Time to Do
Everything on His and Hers Bucket Lists.
May 15, 2017

I have been bothered about the message in that otherwise wonderful movie "La La Land." It's that you can have your great love, or you can follow your dream, but you can't do both.

I just don't want to believe that!

A lot of things divert us from following the path to our vision, but does that mean we can't have a life of love as well as a life of creative fulfillment?

As for me, I chose to postpone my writing dream for a different dream—the life I spent with Lee, raising our kids together. During the years, while enjoying children and grandchildren, I attended writers' conferences off and on. I completed my BA at age 59 and then attained my MFA in creative nonfiction, also dreams of mine.

But still, I didn't write much.

Just, it seemed to me as if all good things would come in their time. That sounds Pollyanna-ish as I type it. And Pollyanna was a fictional character. Probably. Or maybe Eleanor Porter, the author, was indeed that optimistic girl. Eleanor didn't start publishing until she was 45 years old, which was getting up there in 1913. Like me, publishing in my seventies.

Although I'd published this and that, I only began writing for real in 2013. I wanted to write Lee's life story so he could confirm the information I'd learned about him, and also get down the stories he'd told—interweaving mine as well—over our almost 50 years together. Lee did read and approve "You and I and Love Soup"—in manuscript, not book form.

After Lee died, I wanted to write about what has to be done by a widow or widower or executor during the first year ("A Widow's Business"), and then stories about some of the happenings in my life, and then a workbook for recording all the important information in our lives, plus what we want whom to receive, once we're not here to give it ("Rest Assured").

I had a chat with my gynecologist, Mary Jane, the other day. She said it seemed to her that I was taking good care of all parts of my being: health, family, friends, travel, creativity—I was doing it all.

Mary Jane and her husband, both near retirement, had considered that they weren't "doing it all." They've only just drawn up their bucket lists. She laughed because their individual lists do not have a lot in common.

I reassured her that they *can* do it all, his and hers, so long as they accept that they can't—or that they don't have to—do it all at once.

Perhaps there were times in our life when we've felt that we haven't been able do something we want to do because of other commitments and responsibilities. But, think about it. If we freely took on those obligations, then we *are* doing what we want to be doing! And if we're lucky, we will also have time to do the things we set aside.

So maybe I am overly optimistic to believe we can have both, that we can do it all. Or maybe I'm just lucky. Although I've known all my life what I wanted to do creatively, I just wasn't in a hurry to do it. I guess it's about priorities.

I used to profess that I wanted to be a writer but I didn't have anything to say. Now I can barely turn myself off.

And there is still enough love to go around.

• • •

AFTER STORY:
After reading the story, my granddaughter Sally sent me this quotation from her hero, Ruth Bader Ginsburg:

> "You can't have it all, all at once.
> Who—man or woman—has it all, all at once?
> Over my lifespan, I think I have had it all."

That's the spirit!

What the dickens are "fidget spinners"?
July 17, 2017

All of a sudden, I am hearing about them everywhere! Even in the funny papers!

When I first saw the gadgets on the counter, they reminded me of the replacement heads for Norelco shavers. I saw them in Lido Pharmacy on Sunday and ignored them. But Mark was with me, and he asked the woman who was waiting on me what they were.

"They're just . . . things. They spin. Here's an open one."

Mark fidgeted with it but put it down shortly.

I wondered who'd ever want one of those. But as I think back, I have used "fidget devices" most of my life. It's hard for me, for example, to sit still when I am on hold on the telephone. These days, I tend to play Spider solitaire while I'm waiting and checking the clock.

In years past, I had a connected strip of pink and blue blocks that were hinged in such a way that they could be bent into all sorts of shapes, and that kept me distracted from the passing of time. A Rubic's cube could also distract me, although I never had all sides matching at once. (Mark can unscramble a Rubic's cube in less than a minute.)

Before and after those, I've had "magic wands" in various colors.

The magic wands' claim to fame is that the bits of beads and stars and sparkles inside of the hard, narrow plastic capsule slide slowly from one end to the other as you tip an end up. Not awesome, but diverting.

My favorite magic wand is about a foot long and has peach-colored doo-dads in it. If you're in a darkened room, some of the bits inside glow in the dark.

Lee brought back a 6-foot purple magic wand from Hawaii about the time of our 20th anniversary. It held a place of honor on a shelf and was mainly removed to fascinate our littlies—grandchildren and great-grands. In the hall bathroom with the lights turned off, "the stars came out." And the ooohs and aaaahs. It was handed down to Jan who is the grandmother of our great-grandkids.

Some people doodle, some tear paper into confetti, and some now use fidget spinners.

If you see someone holding a flat, sort of triangular metallic thing by its center and spinning it with his or her other hand, that's a fidget spinner. They come in a multitude of colors and some of them seem to cause a blur of color as you spin them.

I've never been one to sit and wait patiently for anything. Sometimes, I find myself nervously playing with the rings I wear on a chain that are usually concealed beneath my sweatshirts. In a doctor's office, I am deep in a book so as not to watch time pass. On the phone, when someone has overestimated the depth of my interest in what they're saying, I am likely to be "magic-wanding," or if I'm on hold, playing Spider solitaire.

I should've bought me one o' them new-fangled things.

• • •

AFTER STORIES:

(1) My daughter Jan bought me a really pretty one for my birthday!

(2) My friend Diana told me that she has a yellow one, which she can set spinning and balance on her nose.

AFTERTHOUGHT:

That (2) reminded me of the time—I was about 50 then—I said, "Look, Daddy! I can balance a spoon on my nose!"

He responded, "Yes, but why would you want to?"

My father usually had a pretty good sense of humor. I wish he were still here so, when Diana teaches me, I could show him that I can balance a fidget spinner on my nose.

Do you *have* to know why you'd want to do that?

I drove into the dealership, but I walked into a cliché.
Cliché, yes, but I really did . . .
July 7, 2017

On Tuesday morning, I was supposed to be at the Newport Beach Tennis Club at 9:45 for a 10:00 ladies' duplicate bridge game with my Encore friends.

When I started up my car, the dashboard read-out said "Replace key battery."

Oh, dear. I've never had a "keyless" ignition before, and I didn't know whether the warning allowed me days or minutes to replace that battery. Worse, I had promised to hurry home to meet the painter after bridge, and I didn't think I would have time to stop at the dealership after bridge.

And what if I *couldn't* return home because my key battery was dead?

I decided to take a chance and stop at the dealership on the way.

"Can you replace my key battery?" I asked the first helper I saw.

"No, ma'am. You have to go to the parts department for that."

"I don't know where that is, and I am in something of a hurry," I said.

"I'll escort you," he said. "It'll take just a few minutes."

I was third in line. A lady getting her key battery replaced was ahead of me, and somebody on the phone was occupying the time of the other parts fellow.

"I've never had a keyless car," I explained, "and I don't know how long I have before I the battery dies."

"You don't need a key battery to drive your car," the parts man said. "You just take this thing here out of that thing there, and you have a key."

Oh, right. When I bought the car almost a year ago, someone had mentioned that.

I wondered how I'm supposed to get that big pushbutton out of the key slot, but I didn't have time to pursue that thought.

The transaction was completed in plenty of time for me to get to the NBTC before 10:00. I found a distant parking place and was rushing along, in my new two-inch sandals, looking into my big purse for my wallet, to get my two-dollar buy-in, when whooosh . . .

I fell down on my *derrière*.

OMG! I couldn't believe my eyes as to what had caused the fall.

Five lovely tennis-playing women came over to help me. I took my shoes off to get some leverage, and bless them, they got me up. I put my shoes back on and assessed the situation.

Just like a slapstick comedian, I had slipped on a banana peel. Not just a banana peel but a whole banana that had been run over in the parking lot.

"Who'd put a banana on the ground like that?" one tennis lady asked.

"It must've fallen out of some kid's backpack," another tennis lady said.

"What a cliché!" I laughed. "I slipped on a banana peel!"

I assured the women I was fine, thanked them for their help, reported the road hazard, and headed for the bridge room.

I thought about that ionic anklet I'd bought at the O.C. Fair that was supposed to help me keep my balance, but I decided not to find fault with it. I don't recall a warranty regarding bananas.

My hands were shaking, although I wasn't hurt or upset. I was just jazzed that I'd slipped on a banana peel, or a banana—same difference—as if I'd walked into a vaudeville routine!

When all was bid and played and tallied, my partner Pauline and I won, and I got home in time to meet the painter.

Was it a lucky/unlucky banana peel? A lucky/unlucky key battery?

When you think about the unliklihood of slipping on a banana peel, the obvious message is "Look where you're going. Even if you're late."

But we all already *know* that!

Learning from experience comes down to realizing that what we *know* doesn't work unless we *use* it.

. ● .

AFTER STORY:
No, really. I didn't even bruise. I think the parking lot must be made of recycled tennis balls. Or my experience of random clumsy falls, throughout my life, has taught me how to land.

ACKNOWLEDGMENTS

Publishers/Editors/Programs
Grace Rachow, *A Community of Voices*
Susan Bono, *Tiny Lights*
John Canalis, *The Daily Pilot*,
a Community Newspaper of *The Los Angeles Times*
Kevin Proff, *Pacific Center OASIS*

Facilitators
Bill Thomas, *Mentor and Motivator*
Patricia Harrelson, MFA, *Editor*
Maura O'Flynn, *Photography*
Lisa Zaharoni, *Photography*
Brian Hillman, *Computer Guru*
And Lee, *My Everything.*

Extra Thanks to:
Tori Hemingson, Ed Frankel,
and my Antioch cohort and professors
who helped me learn to put words together.
And to all the people who read my pieces in the *Daily Pilot*
and encouraged me to keep writing.

Friends Who Let Me Write About Them
The Three Other Citrus Avenue Girls (in 1947-1952)
Jeanne Ragus, Sharon Stahler, Mary Ellyn Oakley
The Encore Women
Other Tolerant Friends
My Family and Extended Family

Thank you, you lovely, generous people!

• • •

A POUND OF EXPERIENCE,
A PINCH OF HUMOR
is also available on Kindle.

Other Books by Liz Swiertz Newman

YOU AND I AND LOVE SOUP:
A Memoir or Two

REST ASSURED:
Preparing a Guide for Your Executor and Heirs

A WIDOW'S BUSINESS:
A Practical Guide Through the First Year
After the Death of a Spouse

Available at

www.amazon.com
and
www.BarnesAndNoble.com
(www.bn.com)

• • • • •

54353491R00149

Made in the USA
San Bernardino, CA
14 October 2017